Pray Without Kidding

Pray Without Kidding

by Jerry F. Dawson

EAKIN PRESS ⬥ Austin, Texas

Library of Congress Cataloging-in-Publication Data

Dawson, Jerry F.
    Pray without kidding / by Jerry F. Dawson.
        p.   cm.
    ISBN 1-57168-342-9
    1. Christian life--Anecdotes. 2. Dawson, Jerry F.--Anecdotes. 3. Baptists--
Texas--Anecdotes. 4. Christian life--Baptist authors. I. Title.
BV4517 D39   1999
248.4'861--dc21   99-047813

DEDICATION

To:
Margie, my unfailing source of joy, inspiration, and
encouragement for nearly fifty years.

And to our wonderful family:

Our son Kim Alden, his wife Sharon, and their son Michael
Our son Carey Austin, his children Cara, Courtney, Brandy,
Emily, and Zachary
Our daughter Jamie Lynn, her husband Steven, and their
children Dawson and Darby

Contents

Foreword

Stories, parables, anecdotes—throughout history people have utilized these to transmit values, ideals, and even history itself from generation to generation. One of the best informed and most skillful communicators in this fashion is Jerry Dawson. Hearing him in all kinds of settings led me to urge him to put this material in print. The result was *Elmer and the Peas and Other Dawsonisms: Inspiration, Satire, and Humor by an Educated Baptist* published by Eakin Press in 1997.

The book enjoyed immediate positive response from a wide variety of persons. For example, Don Newbury, chancellor of Howard Payne University, declared, "He has brightened many days for many thousands with his humor, delivered in the classic Dawson style that borders on the inimitable." And D. L. Lowrie, pastor and noted preacher, wrote, "I commend the book of this friend to you."

The enthusiastic praise and clear appeal to a wide and diverse readership has led to *Pray Without Kidding*.

It will no doubt bring a similar reaction as *Elmer* did as described by Lowrie: "You will laugh, weep, pray, and thank God for His faithfulness."

A dedicated Christian and the product of Baptist life, Dawson draws upon a wide variety of his personal experiences for his stories. Growing up in a West Texas oil town, he knew first hand the rough, dangerous, and exciting life of the oil patch. Part Native American in his ancestry, he saw life a bit differently (he let me know that "circling the wagons" was not one of his favorite expressions!) than some. In his early years his father was a non-Christian bouncer in a bar who later became a devout Baptist deacon (a person whose company I always enjoyed), and this experience helped Dawson see both sides of church life and understand the profound effect of being born again through faith in Jesus Christ. Dawson's own faith journey began through the witness of a Sunday School teacher from a new church and made him appreciate the need for both Sunday Schools and new churches.

As a young man the molding effect of a Baptist school—Wayland Baptist University (then College)—shaped his life for ministry. His intellectual abilities were stimulated and his devotion to Christ deepened. As a result he pursued graduate studies which culminated in a Ph.D. degree from the University of Texas and began a lifetime involvement in preaching and teaching.

Following God's will to the mission field of higher education, he taught history at Wayland Baptist University and Texas A&M University, became dean of the Graduate School at Southwest Texas State University, and served as president of East Texas Baptist University before becoming director of the Christian Education Coordinating Board of the Baptist General Convention of Texas. This later position brought him into constant contact with churches, Baptist schools, and Baptist Student Ministry leaders. He also took part in Partnership Missions in various parts of the world. And interspersed throughout these experiences, he has served more than sixty churches as interim pastor.

Along the way he became a husband, father, and grandfather—all of which added to his repertoire of stories.

Thus some of his accounts are from the history he knows extraordinarily well. Others are from his own numerous and varied life experiences. His deep devotion to Christ and love of the Bible cause him often to apply the stories to Christian faith and Biblical truth. Readers will laugh and cry. They will gain new insight into the Bible and life. They will come to understand themselves and their world better.

So, thank you again, Jerry Dawson, for your continued infectious enthusiasm for life as reflected in this new volume of your stories, anecdotes, and parables.

William M. Pinson, Jr.
Executive Director,
Baptist General Convention of Texas
Dallas, Texas, April 3, 1999

Introduction

Reinhard's Story

I first introduced Reinhard to readers in *Elmer and the Peas,* published in 1997. His was a classic example of the book's premise that everyone's life is filled with stories, anecdotes, and experiences worthy of attention.

We met Reinhard at the International Baptist Church in Stuttgart, Germany, where we were helping in a church family retreat. We might never have become acquainted but for the fact that someone mentioned that it was Reinhard's birthday and led the group in singing a happy birthday salute.

Three "first" impressions emerged from my conversations with Reinhard that night.

First, he was a double for Tom Cruise. He would have lived a life of high adventure on an American college campus.

Second, he had a highly unusual sense of a godly call to live a life of service.

Third, our meeting was not accidental. His was a story I wanted to know.

To make a long story short, a few months later Reinhard accepted our invitation to come to Arlington, Texas, and attend the university, taking a course entitled English As A Second Language. Part of the orientation tour I gave him led us to the office of Tillie Bergin, the heart and soul of a house of miracles known as Mission Arlington.

Before we had departed for Germany a few months earlier, I had paid a visit to Mission Arlington and had chatted briefly with Tillie. She was courteous enough to listen to my prattle about the upcoming mission trip to Germany, but there was obviously something more important on her mind.

"That is all well and good, but I need someone to help

with our puppet ministry. Our leader is leaving," she said with a note of desperation. "Can you help me with this?"

Now, a few months later, Reinhard and I step into Tillie's office to offer his services as a part-time baker for Mission Arlington while he studied at the University of Texas at Arlington, four blocks away.

Before I could share with Tillie the good news about Reinhard's skills as a baker in Germany, she abruptly asked if I had ever found for her a replacement for the puppet ministry.

And before I could say no, Reinhard spoke up.

"I do puppets," he proudly proclaimed.

I shall never forget the exultation of that moment for Tillie, for Reinhard, and for me.

I had thought I was going to Stuttgart to minister to them.

Well, not exactly. I was actually going to Stuttgart to minister to Reinhard and his church, but I was also part of the work of getting him to the U.S.A. to minister to Americans for HIM. Reinhard's story, my story, Tillie's story, and the story for countless Arlington students were all intertwined.

Now for the rest of Reinhard's story.

It had been determined early in his life that Reinhard had no future in academic pursuits. In that rigid educational system so pervasive in Germany, he was relegated to study a trade or vocation rather than prepare for college. To a very great extent he was locked in to this track for the rest of his life.

Then came the course in English As A Second Language. Reinhard completed the course of study at the head of the class, and with this accomplishment came the realization that he could succeed in academic areas which he previously had assumed were beyond his grasp.

It might be said that he caught the "American Dream."

Upon Reinhard's return to Germany, he was granted admission to the counseling program at the University of Hamburg.

Four years later, Margie and I just "happened" to be in Hamburg the September day in 1997 when he was to begin his final examinations for certification as a professional counselor.

Reinhard passed his exams with flying colors.

Where is he now?

(Please do not shout at this point in his story.)

He is working with children of migrants seeking citizenship in Germany. This social service is part of the national immigration program. The institution which has been given the oversight of this wonderful work is the Baptist Church of Hannover.

I thought that I had gone to Germany to minister, only to find that I was really going to find Reinhard so that he could help in Mission Arlington. Or had I actually gone to Germany to get Reinhard to bring him to the U.S. so that he could be equipped to go back to Germany to work with children at the Baptist Church of Hannover?

Or . . .?

It is a distinct possibility that the story is currently unfinished. Someday, in the fullness of time, someone may step forward and tell of the strange coincidence that brought Reinhard into his or her life in a land far from home and made a change in that person's eternal life.

Hopefully, readers of these very lines may find it appropriate to look for the stories, finished and unfinished, in their own lives.

Pray Without Ceasing

The great lessons of life are not always learned as the direct result of doing something "bad." Often they are learned as a direct result of doing "good" things badly.

One of the truly good pages from my life bears the heading of First Baptist Church of Lubbock, Texas. In 1966 I had the rewarding privilege of serving there as interim pastor and that in turn developed into a continuing love affair that has resulted in assorted invitations to return from time to time.

Many of the "good" experiences of my life are directly related to service at Lubbock, but I have to qualify things a bit by confessing that not all good experiences produced good results.

In 1972, while I was serving Southwest Texas State University as graduate dean, I accepted one of those "routine" invitations to speak at First Baptist Church for both Sunday services. The invitation was sweetened a bit by the news that I would be the guest of Dan and Jeanne Law over the weekend.

Great! A short Saturday evening flight to Lubbock, a weekend in the home of wonderful friends, a reunion with many of our dearest fellow Baptists, and then another short flight out late Sunday evening. Everything seemed to point toward a great experience.

Things proceeded in a routine manner until I presented my ticket at the terminal in Austin for my one-hour flight to Lubbock. It seems that there was a misprint on the advance purchase ticket. The flight number was correct, but the point of departure was incorrect. As we were speaking, my flight was taking off from San Antonio.

After exploring every option, it was apparent that the only choice open to me was to drive to Lubbock. I routinely called Margie and told her that I was headed toward Lubbock and would probably get there about 2:00 A.M. Then I called Dan Law and shared my change of plans with them, securing in return the assurance that the back door would be unlocked and that I should make myself at home in the guest bedroom.

Being the good friends that they were, the Laws let me sleep as late as possible before waking me for a quick breakfast and speedy departure for the 8:30 A.M. service at First Baptist Church. And in the haste toward punctuality, it actually passed through my mind that I perhaps should call Margie and let her know that I had made it safely to Lubbock and all was well.

I would do that. Right after the conclusion of the early service!

But, of course, when the time arrived to call, I realized that Margie and the kids would be in church at San Marcos. The call would have to wait until early afternoon. But the afternoon gave way to a small gathering of friends who wanted to renew old memories, and the only option was a late night call. And this plan was altered after a post-service fellowship caused us to get back to the Laws about 11:00 P.M.

Too late for a call. How about Monday for sure?

At this point my good friend Dan Law offered one last enticement to "top off" a great weekend. Dan, Junior Arturburn, and Pete Claytor had scheduled a quail hunt for Monday morning at Jack Kirkpatrick's ranch near Post. Why not join them, since I had to go that way on my way back to San Marcos?

It was late Monday afternoon when we all assembled around the cleaning barrel at Jack's ranch to dress our quail that I suddenly had a moment of inspiration—I needed to call

Margie and let her know that I might be a little late getting home that night.

At the conclusion of a good weekend of good preaching (assumed), good fellowship with good people, good reunions with good friends, a good day of recreation with good hunting buddies, and good intentions beyond measure, I placed a collect call to my good family in San Marcos.

Imagine my surprise when the operator informed me that my party had indicated she would not accept a collect call from me. Period!

All of a sudden, I was overwhelmed with a sense of urgency about going home. (I still do not know what the guys did with my share of the bird hunt.) And it should not come as a surprise that I did not get sleepy on the trip home.

A late arrival (2:00 A.M.), followed by a very cool reception (everyone was sound asleep), was followed by an even colder scene at the breakfast table. It was almost a relief when the phone rang, and Margie at least had to say "Hello."

The voice on the other end could easily be heard to say, "Mrs. Dawson, this is Dan Law's Marriage Counseling Service. I understand that you may be in need of my services today."

Only then did I learn that Margie had taken the initiative the day before and had called to learn if I were in fact among the living or the dead, and if living, the soon to die.

I had been so busy doing "good" that I had neglected to observe the simplest of obligations. I had failed to keep contact with "home" because of the busy schedule of my good works.

And why should I be surprised about my failures in calling home? I had often paid even less attention to calling "home" to the Heavenly Father.

At the rate I was going, it would not be surprising if the Father flatly refused to accept my next "collect call."

Doing "good" and "calling Home" really ought to go together.

Paul urged us to *"pray without ceasing"* (I Thessalonians 5:17). The absence of prayer leads to doing good things badly.

Pray Without Kidding

Paul advised the believers in Thessolonica to pray without ceasing. For modern day saints he might well have added, "pray without kidding."

Probably no element of the Christian faith is bandied about as recklessly and carelessly as the term "prayer." And probably no part of the Christian community is more casual about the term than are those who lead their congregations. The problem with loose references to prayer is that folks have a tendency to remember statements about prayer as though they were solemn promises from the pulpit.

When I served First Baptist Church in Dimmitt, Texas, as interim pastor in the 1960s, I was exposed for the first time to intensive irrigation farming on a massive scale. Dimmitt was in the very center of a vast farming complex that required enormous equipment, huge capital investment, and superhuman effort. I honestly believe that the congregation of that church included the hardest working individuals I have ever served as pastor.

I quickly noticed that attendance was pretty meager for Wednesday night prayer services. When I asked where everyone was, someone informed me that folks deemed it important to spend the last hours of daylight "in the fields."

The next Sunday morning I concluded services with a word of encouragement to participate in prayer services on Wednesday night.

"Folks," I said, "If you don't come on to church on Wednesday night for prayer meeting, I am going to pray for rain on Wednesday afternoons about five o'clock. It will be too wet to work, and you'll have to come to church."

I laughed at the obvious exaggeration, and the people responded with a good-natured chuckle, but I immediately sensed that I had touched a very sensitive nerve. Those folks did not want rain of any kind in October, period!

Good thing we all knew that I was just kidding.

The next Wednesday afternoon, a strange weather change

was accompanied by a brief but significant two-inch downpour. It began raining about 5:00 P.M.

The fun started about 7:00 P.M. As folks came into the prayer service, any number of them said, "Well, you said you would get it to rain about five."

They laughed, but somehow it did not seem all that funny.

One week later, about 5:00 P.M., it rained! At prayer service, several folks mentioned that once was plenty, and precious few people laughed.

The third Wednesday night service was preceded by a two-inch downpour. It was not accompanied by any form of levity at all in the prayer service at 7:00 P.M. More than a few fine folks mentioned to me that "enough was enough," and it was time to "cut it out."

One must remember at this point that, with irrigated crops grown in dense rows, it took at least a good week to get over a rain. It thus had been several weeks of costly idleness since I had off-handedly suggested that I would pray for rain.

If one can comprehend all of this, one can easily see my problem when, for the fourth consecutive Wednesday afternoon, it rained.

I have never felt so apologetic in my entire life. I was on the verge of assuring the congregation that the Father had never answered a single prayer in my life.

Several months later the church called Frank Pollard as pastor. He confessed to me much later that he was amazed at the questions put to him during the interview process with the Pastor Search Committee. In particular, it struck him as peculiar when he was asked about his theological position on rain.

Which Way is the Library?

The era of Vietnam protests on college and university campuses made permanent impressions on everyone involved —faculty, administration, students, parents, the public.

Probably no other historical event in American history caused such pervasive pain, anguish, and hatred that were part of the daily life at most American educational institutions in the 1960s and 1970s.

I still remember the sick feeling that came over me when I looked at the ashes of the main administrative building at Colorado State University in Fort Collins. Some said that the demise of this stately educational symbol started with angry high school students who were protesting the use of grapes in the fruit salad being served to them at a banquet.

More tragic was viewing the ashes of once productive lives of students who had decided to "check out" of the system they associated with the Vietnam conflict. The nation is still suffering the loss of these potential contributors to a better way of life for their generation.

Not all of the memories traceable to this troubled era are grim. Some were the result of that funny part of human nature that does stupid things in the name of worthy causes.

My doctoral studies and a considerable segment of my teaching career centered on events in the various German states during and after the era of the French Revolution. It struck me as more than a coincidence that German students had played a critical role in the War of Liberation in spite of their determination to open German society to a new nationalistic fervor which was adamantly opposed by the conservative leadership of the German states.

When I suggested to Dr. Milton Nance, head of the History Department at Texas A&M, that research into the topic, and the possible implications for our contemporary scene, might be valuable, he concurred. I narrowed the research sites to Harvard and the University of Colorado. The excellent nineteenth-century collection of German periodicals available at Boulder finally sealed my determination to pursue the topic further. I requested, and was granted, a research grant from my dean's office at Texas A&M to look into the topic during leave time in 1970.

Little did I know that events were taking place on the University of Colorado campus which would make my days there a permanent storehouse of agonizing experiences.

It seems that word had spread along the "Hippie" information network that a sort of national Hippie convention should take place on the campus during the summer of 1970.

By the time I arrived for my initial visit to the university, at least ten thousand card-carrying Hippies were there to greet me. They made the magnificent grassy mall in the center of the campus their rallying point and filled every square inch of that space with a uniform mass of humanity.

Having never been to the library, I inadvertently parked about as far as possible from the library that overlooked the masses and the mall.

Wearing my best dark suit, sporting a standard Aggie "look" (close cut hair, clean shave, shined shoes), and carrying the omnipresent black brief case, I turned a corner of the economics building and found myself standing in front of two college age males.

What I saw were standard, run-of-the-mill Hippies.

What they saw was a cop, a campus security officer, or something roughly equivalent.

They immediately shook off that sleepy, blank, what's-happening-man look and jumped to attention.

Hence the following conversation:

"Hi, fellows," I said as cheerfully as possible. "You students here?"

The response was immediate. It was almost like an old western movie where the "bad guys" go for their guns. In this case, the Hippies went for their ID cards.

"YES SIR," they responded in unison as they magically produced clean, shiny, new student identification cards attesting to their status as students at Boulder. I might add that the cards were the only clean items in the possession of either person.

Holding his evidence only a few inches from my face, the spokesman for the two added, "I am a sophomore here. I love this wonderful school."

"Great. Could you kindly point out to me the library?" I asked.

I might just as well have asked for a recitation of Lincoln's

Gettysburg Address. An absolutely incredulous look flickered across his face.

He spread his arms as wide as possible and assured me, "Man, it is BIG! **BIG!**"

It was all I could do to keep from laughing out loud.

I responded, "I'm sure it is a big building. But which building is it?"

By this time his friend had managed to hide behind him, becoming almost an identical shadow, but the maneuver did not save him.

"My buddy here can tell you where it is. He has been a student here longer than I have," he assured me.

"Wonderful!" I said.

I could almost put the words in his mouth for him, but it was worth the wait to let him say them himself.

"It is REALLY BIG," he assured me, spreading his arms and then rolling them in circles.

A casual glance across the campus on my part settled which building obviously housed my reason for being at Boulder, and I parted company with those two long-term, semi-permanent members of the student body. I laughed halfway across the mall.

> If someone asks us for directions concerning the Kingdom of God, we can usually produce some kind of evidence that we "belong."

Then the irony of the moment struck me. Those two fellows were not all that different from average church members.

If someone asks us for directions concerning the Kingdom of God, we can usually produce some kind of evidence that we "belong." Most of us would end up describing our Lord as "Big." We wear the uniform, almost look alike, and blend in with the group.

We salute symbols of the Father's authority, but most of the time we have to turn to someone else to provide even the most fundamental information about how to find the Father.

We may not be taking advantage of the vast resources available to us, but at least we are not causing any trouble.

A Man of Unclean Lips

The research library at the University of Colorado was a marvelous testimony to man's desire to preserve his culture in the printed word. I also came to treasure it as a refuge from the broiling masses of counterculture people who had assembled by the thousands on the vast, grass-covered mall in front of the building.

I shall never forget the feeling of revulsion I felt when I emerged from my first visit to the library. At first I saw all ten thousand people. It was like looking at a grandstand at a football game and seeing everyone, but focusing on no one person in particular.

It was when I really started looking closely that I saw the little "love" children in every manner of undress, uncleanness, and uncombed hair. I immediately resented the fact that children were being treated like the German shepherd dogs that every "couple" seemed to have.

I saw every personal biological urge being met by a pointedly anti-social public act. It was almost like a sacrilegious act designed to produce maximum shock value.

A haze from the unnumbered marijuana cigarettes hung like a cloud over the entire gathering, and one could only guess at what was being passed from person to person and lifted to the nostrils. There was every manner of dress and undress. It was almost like a giant enactment of some pagan ritual from the Old Testament.

I almost prayed the prayer of the Pharisee who said to God, *"Lord, I thank thee that I am not like these people."* With my suit, briefcase, credentials, haircut, and conscience it would not have been hard to be thankful that I was indeed different from these people.

It was when I pictured myself as being so different from the throng of ten thousand Hippies that I developed a sense of despair.

If I felt revulsion at the ugliness of man, how much more would God be troubled by what He saw in me? I was more like than unlike the people I was judging.

Only then I remembered the words of Isaiah when he said, *"Lord I am a man of unclean lips, and I dwell in the midst of a land of unclean lips."*

I'm still unsure as to the whole truth I encountered that day. I just knew that if God disliked Hippies as much as I did at that moment, then *I was the one* in real trouble.

And Lo, He Has Ascended

The so-called Hippie Era left scars, memories, feelings, and emotions which defy retelling. The lost lives, the explosion of reliance upon drugs, the massive disillusionment with the political process—all left marks on those who lived through the Vietnam experience.

When asked about their personal involvement in, or memories about, this double decade of social unrest, most people find it difficult to escape a weighty feeling of loss. When recalling their experiences, most folks assume the posture of a casual observer rather than an active participant.

My most poignant recollection of the entire era holds a mixture of sadness and humor.

The annual meeting of the Western Historical Association was about to conclude with a plenary session in a large hotel in Denver. The topic for the plenary session was "Religion in the West," and the panel of commentators read like a Who's Who in American religion.

Only a few minutes into the session, a hush fell over the audience as the attention of those seated on the platform became fixed upon a young man standing just inside the entrance to the hall.

The object of their attention was wearing a long white robe, had long flowing hair, and sported a cleanly trimmed beard.

Our unannounced visitor seemed to have come directly from a painted wall in Milan.

If so, the trip had seemingly dazzled him, for his eyes had a very distant look about them.

In his hands he held a short length of rope with a large knot tied in each end. When a complete hush fell upon the crowd, our visitor raised his right hand in a manner right out of the Vatican. He seemed to be the only person in the audience of over five hundred historians who was not utterly speechless.

Then came six words I shall remember forever.

"It is I. Be not afraid!"

It struck me that if he were really who he thought he was, he could have been a little more original. He had already used that expression once.

At this awkward moment of embarrassing silence, the dean of Catholic educators in America left the platform and made his way directly to the robed messenger standing transfixed with arm aloft. With incredible gentleness he embraced the young man, and then the two turned and left the hall together.

He returned alone in a minute or two and made his way back to the platform.

"I have escorted our visitor to the elevator, and LO, HE HAS ASCENDED," he proclaimed.

Sensing that his next words to this gathering of religious scholars might carry the weight of immortality, he added, "When I left work to come to the meeting, the last person I expected to see was THE BOSS."

Unfortunately, it can be said of most of us that the last person we expect to see on any given day is THE BOSS.

Why Not Tonight?

Stories abound about the gunfighters in the days of the old West. Usually most of the accounts end up with a hero and an outlaw facing each other in a frozen glare. Finally, one little twitch by one of the two sets off a wild and noisy series of desperate moves.

Used car salesmen tell somewhat the same story about "signs" to look for in the face of the prospective buyer that indicate it is time to "go for it."

On a larger plain, televised debates between Nixon and Kennedy made a lasting imprint on the style of campaign debates. It became apparent that a glance, a gesture, or a blush can change the course of history and the destiny of a nation.

It all seems to come down to communication as an art form as well as a personal response.

The early church recognized the special role played by non-verbal communication. Signs, stained glass windows, relics, special clothing, and icons all found a place as a part of the worship experience.

Therefore, it should not be surprising that there is a constant apprehension that forms of worship should not take the place of substance. Just a brief scan of televised religious experiences will convince even the most critical observer that contemporary worship leaders have mastered the art of communicating effectively.

Recently we attended a funeral service for a relative. The family of the deceased was evenly divided between the Catholic and Baptist faith.

At the very outset of the service the priest introduced himself and noted that much of what was about to take place would seem foreign to nearly half of the audience. Some elements of the service had to do with traditions, some related to the scriptures, and some were the result of special requests.

In a matter of three minutes he made it possible for everyone in attendance to understand and appreciate the entire service. It was a masterful example of great communication.

It should also be noted that the modern church also provides classic examples of the breakdown in communication. Unfortunately, we have a tendency to remember those hilarious flubs that tend to overshadow an entire service. My first is the most lasting.

We were in revival services in Field, New Mexico. Our group was called the Volunteer Mission Band and consisted of eight students from Wayland Baptist College. We were short on experience and long on self-confidence.

The weekend of activities and services were to culminate with a climactic and powerful evangelistic service with the congregation of twenty members of the Baptist church.

Congregational music, a solo, a duet, and a personal testimony led up to my sermon, "Now is the time. This is the appointed hour."

When you are nineteen years old, you pick topics like that.

It also takes forty-five minutes to say it.

My last point was the same as my first point. Today is the day. Now is the hour. Change your life NOW!

> Thank goodness our Lord is not entirely dependent upon human perfection to get His message across.

When I reached the elusive moment of closure for the sermon, I turned to Tommy, our song leader on the team.

"Brother Tommy," I said. "What are we going to sing for our hymn of invitation?"

Evidently my eloquence had moved him into a deep state of contemplation, or else he was asleep with his eyes wide open. Obviously surprised by my question, he bolted into action. He grabbed his *Modern Hymnal,* and scanned his memory for the number of an appropriate song to use.

"Number 388," he responded with fire and thunder.

It only took fifteen seconds for pandemonium to break loose. Even some members of our team had the audacity to laugh.

Hymn 388 was entitled, "Oh Why Not Tonight?"

Needless to say, the service was over.

Thank goodness our Lord is not entirely dependent upon human perfection to get His message across.

One Little Word

Every day we are reminded of the power inherent in the use of words.

You can fill a pretty good-sized library with books devoted to the implications, court decisions, and constitutional problems that have resulted from the use of the word "person" in one amendment to the U.S. constitution after the Civil War.

Wars have erupted, dynasties have fallen, empires have been shaken due to the use, misuse, or abuse of seemingly simple words.

The expression "I do," can do more to alter fifty years of one's life than any other thing said in his or her lifetime.

In spite of the demonstrated implications of any and every thing we say or write, most of us live as though words have an effect on "them" but not "us." I learned my own lesson about this the hard way.

I completed my doctoral dissertation in October of 1963 and received my doctor of philosophy diploma at the University of Texas in the spring commencement ceremonies in 1964. As an aside to the graduation ceremony, I was impressed by the fact that President and Mrs. Lyndon Johnson also received doctorates, albeit honorary.

Between the completion of the dissertation and the graduation ceremony, I was invited to present the basic elements of my dissertation, *The Evolution of Friedrich Schleiermacher as a Nationalist,* at a plenary session of the Southern Historical Society meeting in Ashville, North Carolina.

Had I had known that Boyd Shafer was in the audience when I presented my paper, I would have been terrified. Not only was he a dominant personality in the American Historical

Association and the *American Historical Review,* he was the leading American authority on the topic of European nationalism. I had cited his works a number of times in my own studies on German nationalism.

After the program, Shafer congratulated me on the presentation and expressed interest in my research.

One cannot imagine how flattered I was to receive a letter from Shafer after receiving my degree. He wanted to read my dissertation!

The request was more complex than it first appears. I had made an original and two carbon copies of my dissertation, and that was before the magic of the Xerox machine.

The original was filed at the Graduate Office of the University of Texas. Dr. John Rath had been given the customary first carbon. My copy was the only other in existence.

It constituted an act of great faith for me to send Boyd Shafer my "only child."

Months passed, and then the mail produced my copy of the dissertation and a letter containing both good news and bad.

First, the good news. He liked my dissertation.

Second, the bad news. He outlined several single-spaced pages of alterations that he felt would enhance the quality and readability of the manuscript.

My response was to send a note of thanks to Dr. Shafer, and put Mr. Schleiermacher on the shelf.

After six months of "putting it off," I turned again to the suggestions and began in earnest the revision of my original manuscript in the light of Shafer's suggestions.

About the time I completed the exhaustive task, I received a letter from the director of the University of Texas Press, expressing an interest in seeing a copy of my doctoral dissertation.

The dream of every historian was about to become a reality.

I responded by sending a bright, shiny revision. In turn, the University of Texas Press informed me that in accordance with their practice they had sent the manuscript to a noted authority in my field to determine its worthiness.

To whom had they sent it?

Boyd Shafer!

He, in turn, recommended it for publication "as is."

All of this is to say that I was about to place my work before the historical world. I wanted it to be right. My editor was determined to assist me in making the book something in which both I and the University of Texas Press would take pride.

All of my conscious memory of the publication process boils down to one word.

Alfred G. Pundt authored an excellent study of the life of Ernst Moritz Arndt, which he entitled, *Arndt and the Nationalist Awakening in Germany.*

When I read the first proof text sent by my editor, I noticed that the word *Nationalist* had been shortened to *National.*

A note called to my attention the fact that the appropriate change had been made at the press.

I immediately dashed off a correction to the correction, calling their attention to the fact that the word Nationalist might seem awkward, but it was in fact the correct word in Pundt's title.

When the second proof copy arrived with the admonition that this was the last opportunity for corrections, I noted with alarm that my request for a change in Pundt's title had not been made. I immediately penciled in the change and then placed a call to the editor.

Once again I readily admitted to the editor that the correct spelling of Nationalist was not a matter of taste or choice. That was the word used, and I had faithfully cited it. Would the editor please see that the correction was given immediate attention?

It was one of the most satisfying days in my educational career when my book, *Friedrich Schleiermacher: The Evolution of a Nationalist*, arrived in the mail.

It was not a perfect piece of work. Through the years I have found a number of things about it that I wish I had changed or omitted. That day the only concern I had was **the word.**

There it was. Big as life. National. And it was WRONG!

Okay, so it was misspelled. There was nothing I could do about it. Besides, I reasoned, who would ever notice it anyway. After all, it was not the end of the world. *Et cetera, et cetera, et cetera.*

The next big hurdle was the *American Historical Review.* Six months after publication, the *Review* sent the book to an authority in the field of nationalism for review and printed the review for all of the historical community to see.

Who was the noted authority to whom they sent *Friedrich Schleiermacher?*

You guessed it. Alfred G. Pundt!

I have always taken pride in Dr. Pundt's mostly complimentary review. The only pain I experienced? It was when he noted that he felt compelled to point out the consistent misspelling of the title of his own book.

Does it seem trite to point out that every word we write or speak is ultimately sent for review to the author of all words? *"For in the beginning was the Word, and the Word was with God, and the Word was God."*

J. Wesley Smith

J. Wesley Smith is a revered name among those who know and treasure the rich heritage of East Texas Baptist University.

For more than three decades he furnished leadership to the College of Marshall and East Texas Baptist College. He was a professor, dean, and acting president. When the school closed its doors in 1926, he personally led a drive to reopen the school, which proved to be the salvation of the institution.

One of the first personal visits I made after arriving at East Texas Baptist College in 1976 was to the modest home of Dr. Smith only two blocks from the campus. Many members of the staff and administration were fearful that Dr. Smith might not live much longer, and their fears were well founded. Dr. Smith passed away shortly thereafter, following his move to California to be with loved ones.

I was the loser in not knowing more of the life, service, and sacrifice of this gentleman.

I actually came to know him more intimately when his family sent for his personal things still at the school. I combed the files for letters, papers, and memorabilia which gave me the vantage point of peering over his shoulder as he poured out his soul on behalf of the school, the faculty, and the students.

Among the artifacts and paper trails which were sent to his descendants in California was one particular letter which is a classic affirmation of the role of Christian education in the lives of seemingly ordinary people.

The letter originated with a concerned mother in Bloomberg, Texas.

It seems that the mother had brought her daughter to Marshall to see if the school and her daughter were compatible.

After "looking over the prospects" and meeting several of the young men on the campus, the mother had concluded that her daughter could probably find better "opportunities" elsewhere.

The files contained no response from J. Wesley Smith. But across the bottom of the letter were written several names. They obviously had been written in ink by the unmistakably shaky hand of Dr. Smith. After each name was a bold exclamation mark.

Pure conjecture tells one that Dr. Smith had done a little detective work and had come up with the names of the young men considered by the mother to be such poor prospects for her daughter.

The first has had a notable career in law before serving as a judge and then had been elected to congress from Marshall.

The second had just announced his approaching retirement as president of Texaco.

The third was a district judge in an adjoining county in East Texas.

The fourth was a federal judge in Texarkana.

The fifth name was hardly legible but resembled that of a successful attorney in Linden.

The last name referred to a student who ultimately became chief executive for a national pipeline company.

I sometimes think about this letter when I try to visualize the twelve men Jesus recruited to be his followers and bear the burden of spreading the Gospel. And to a degree, we get the same impression when we look in the mirror and try to visualize our own future in his Kingdom.

By the way, I would love to know whom that young lady finally married.

Pay Attention To What You Are Saying

One of the privileges of living in the world of Academe is that of hearing some of the finest public speakers in the world.

One of the drawbacks of living in the world of Academe is that of hearing some of the finest public speakers in the world.

Just when you think that there is only a fine line separating the best speakers from the rest, there comes along that speaker so skilled that you remember the speech forever.

Dr. Ed Boles, pastor of First Baptist Church in Beaumont and a highly acclaimed public speaker, was chosen by the senior class of East Texas Baptist College to be the speaker for the spring commencement ceremony.

It can be truthfully asserted that every person in the auditorium, with only one exception, paid undivided attention to every word spoken by the guest speaker. Strangely enough the one person who was not paying attention provides the substance for the speaker's claim to greatness.

Dr. Boles was seated next to me and holding in his hand a manila folder which was clearly identified by a tab which carried in bold type the title, COMMENCEMENT SPEECHES.

At the appropriate time in the program he rose in regal splendor, walked to the podium in complete command, and opened his folder.

From my vantage point directly behind and to one side of the podium, I could plainly see a sheaf of yellow legal size sheets with capitalized words triple spaced.

Dr. Boles immediately demonstrated the accuracy of the accolades he had earned as a public speaker. He moved smoothly and flawlessly from introductory humor to a story about the rigors of college life and the rewards of finishing the task of education.

By the time he had turned two pages, he was into his stride and was clearly the master of the minds and imaginations of everyone present.

Then he turned the third yellow legal size sheet and stopped. He was looking at a white, double-spaced letter size sheet of paper which obviously did not belong with the rest of the material he had already presented.

Only two people in the entire auditorium were in a position to know what was transpiring. Both of us seemed curious as to what was about to happen.

One thing was obvious. It was evident that Dr. Boles had not been paying full attention to what he was saying to the audience. He probably was the only person in the auditorium who did not know what he had just said to them.

Then came the finest demonstration of "pulpit management" I have ever witnessed.

He paused as though suddenly searching his memory for a long-lost fact, saying that he was reminded of a humorous experience that demonstrated his intended goal for the entire presentation. Without missing a beat, he began to tell the listeners a story from a graduation ceremony many years ago.

And while he told his story, he began to go back to the previous page of notes to find out where he was. Reading and talking simultaneously lies in a very special realm of undivided attention, and he was up to the challenge.

By the time he completed his story he had found his place in his prepared text and had moved three white sheets of unwanted speech to the back of his folder. In their place he lined up the rest of his material and proceeded through those pages as though nothing had occurred.

So far as the audience was concerned, the only thing that

had happened was the presentation of an outstanding speech to which one could justifiably devote undivided attention.

They were almost right.

It strikes me that a great many of us could afford to stop ever so often in our Christian experience and "see where we are."

Presidential Perspicacity

The modern day college or university is one of the last vestiges of medieval times in the contemporary world.

Convocation, marking the official opening of the academic year, is probably predated only by the marriage ceremony as an organized social activity.

Latin has a revered status, even though many recipients of the B.A. degree cannot spell baccalaureate.

Police officers and university deans share a common *last resort* and use a mace for crowd control.

And then there is the gown. Ever notice that there is hardly a universal urge on the part of men to appear in public in gowns?

I served as director of the Christian Education Coordinating Board of the Baptist General Convention of Texas for nearly twelve years. My mission was to coordinate the work of the Convention with eight Texas Baptist universities and one academy.

Dr. Ed Rogers served along side me as director of the Human Welfare Coordinating Board and devoted a great deal of his time to the coordination of Convention work with Texas Baptist hospitals.

When asked about the difference between the CECB and the HWCB, I generally replied that with the CECB, all the gowns opened down the front.

Presidential Stuff

The peculiar nature of the collegiate environment makes it possible for students to spend a considerable portion of their adult life in pursuit of an endless series of degree programs and degrees, culminating with an offer to teach the subject matter of said degrees, and never having to go into the real world to test the validity of the yellowed lecture notes accumulated along the way.

Not surprisingly, the loftiest, and often looniest, conceptual holdovers of medieval behavior revolve around the hallowed office of the president.

My granddaughter Cara gave me the most definitive example of this when she was five years old. She spent a day on the East Texas Baptist University campus and posed for what must have seemed an endless series of photos. Everyone seemed to feel compelled to take her picture with me and then ask her how it felt to have a pawpaw who was president.

A week later she paid a visit to her other grandparents and felt a specific obligation to share with them every detail of her very special visit to the campus. She concluded the vivid description by a simple remark about her grandfather.

"He is president, you know," she said.

"Of what?" they asked.

"The United States, of course!" she replied.

The Most Lasting Impressions

If kids blur the lines a bit, one should not be surprised that presidents do, too. Fortunately for all concerned, there are constant reminders that "taint so."

For instance, the Southern Association of Colleges and Schools in Atlanta is the "Holy Ground" to which all Southern presidents make a regular pilgrimage. Accreditation is the com-

mon ground that unites presidents of major universities, regional universities, trade schools, professional schools, liberal arts
colleges, junior colleges, etc., into one big interest group.

One might wonder what the presidents of these various
types, sizes, specialties, and regions could possibly have in
common.

More to the point, what could major state universities
have in common with small denominational liberal arts colleges?

At one of the "presidents only" sessions of SACS in the
eighties, the 1,300-plus body was asked to write on a survey
sheet the last three problems requiring their time before they
left to come to the SACS meeting.

To the amazement of most, the SACS director announced
at the subsequent session that there had been a ninety percent
correlation for three specific problems.

1. The Student Newspaper
2. Faculty Parking
3. Cafeteria Service

Medieval or Mid-level?

The great medieval leveling influence that most presidents
forget about for a while, and then abruptly rediscover, is the
class structure of the faculty. This is true in spite of the fact
that most presidents find their way through the medieval university structure to become chief executive. How soon they
forget.

Six years ago I was contacted by the chair of a university
search committee. His institution was in the process of replac-
ing a fine man who had served them well for a decade. The
school has a fine reputation, and they were anticipating a careful and selective search.

The caller, a friend from days past, said that the committee had a particular person in mind, but in the funny world of

presidential searches they did not feel comfortable in making a direct contact. The prospect had taken early retirement three years before, and the search committee needed to know if he might have an interest in returning to that level of responsibility.

Since we were known to be acquaintances, would it be possible, he asked, for me to contact the person as a "disinterested third party" to see if he had any interest in returning to the presidency. No names were to be used.

This is not that unusual a request, and I readily agreed to perform this task. When I called my friend and gingerly moved the topic to whether or not he might like to "get back in the harness," he went right to the heart of the matter.

"Let's see. I am fifty-seven," he mused. "Eight more years. That means ninety-six meetings with the Music Department before retirement."

Then there was a moment of silence, followed by "Naw, I don't think so."

Never Have I Seen Such Devotion

My first experiences as a public speaker began shortly after I accepted my first appointment as a college professor at Wayland Baptist College in 1960.

A combination of high visibility, a natural scarcity of available speakers, and my inability to say "no" soon led to a full calendar and a lot of conflicts.

Actually, I had the easy part. It was Margie, Kim, Carey, and Jamie who were constantly having to "understand" my absence and adjust to my crazy schedules.

The ultimate test came when I accepted an invitation for a full week of revival services in Fabens, Texas, for the last week in August. Bud Goodwin, one of my recently graduated history majors from Wayland, had prevailed upon me to help him in a major effort to bring new life to the church.

It is a LONG bus ride from Fabens, just outside El Paso, to Plainview. That was a minor inconvenience compared to the problem of getting from the bus station to my house in the late hours of the night.

Taxi service was out of the question. It would be well past bedtime for our nine-year-old, our eight-year-old, and our seven-year-old. It was time for Margie to work her magic and come to my rescue.

Two of our best friends, Don and Susie Tatum, lived next to us. Susie would be getting off her shift at the hospital at about the right time, and Don agreed to stay up and watch both families of kids until (1) Susie got home (2) Margie got back from the station (3) something else happened.

It was the "something else" that is the focus of this narrative.

Margie put the kids to bed, waited until nearly midnight, slipped on her robe, and set out for the worst moment in her whole life.

The bus station was adjacent to the old Hilton Hotel, part of the original chain of hotels that formed the basis for the Hilton empire. Margie parked the car in front of the hotel and waited for my arrival.

She noticed that a police car made a slow pass, but thought nothing of it. A few minutes later the car returned, moving more slowly.

Finally the prowl car stopped next to her, and an officer approached with a flashlight in hand.

"Evening," he said with a note of irritation in his voice. "I don't believe I have seen you around here before. Are you new?"

The voice of honest innocence responded.

"Oh, no," she said. "I'm just waiting on my husband."

The officer stepped back, stood straight and tall, and made an awkward effort at saluting her.

"Never have I seen such devotion!" he asserted as he turned and walked back to his car.

Three observations linger after the fact:

(1)   Be careful how you take compliments from folks;

(2)   Things are not always as they seem;
(3)   Take a cab.

Come to the Cockpit

Someone said that we are fortunate if we develop one good and lasting friendship that stands all the grueling tests of a lifetime.

I count myself fortunate, indeed, that I can number a long list of wonderful people whose friendship I treasure.

Way up close to the top of that list would be the names of Bob and Mary Jean Hazlett.

We met in 1966 while I served as interim pastor at First Baptist Church in Lubbock.

Fortunately, ours has never been the type of friendship that required daily attention, for we have passed through, in, and around various moves and career changes that have always brought us back together.

The Hazletts went with us on a mission trip to Stuttgart, where his rank of lieutenant colonel blended beautifully with a predominately American military congregation.

A short while later he drove four hundred miles so that he and Mary Jean could wash dishes while we worked our way through my father's heart attack and subsequent death.

They are that kind of friends.

It was only natural that we turned to the Hazletts for help when we put together a Partnership Mission trip to the Wollongong Baptist Church in New South Wales, Australia.

One of the inducements that helped Bob to commit time and money to make such a trip was the connection he had developed with the pilots of Qantas Airlines. Bob was serving as regional office manager for the FAA in the Dallas/Fort Worth area and through the years had personally conducted the certification process needed to clear Qantas pilots who made flights to and from the U.S.A.

When the mission team boarded the Qantas flight in Los Angeles for departure to Sydney, it really came as no surprise that the captain recognized Bob. Bob had personally supervised his certification process making him eligible to fly to and from the USA.

There was obvious pride on the part of all our team when the captain came on the speaker and announced that we were fortunate to have his mentor on board and invited him to come to the cockpit. We were further impressed when applause followed Bob up the aisle and back again after a couple of hours "up front."

Two days later it was my privilege to introduce our mission team to the congregation at Wollongong. It was at that point that I realized that I had never had the privilege of introducing Bob Hazlett to any group or gathering.

Fresh from the experience on the plane, I felt that I had the perfect opportunity to establish rapport between the team and the church by telling them about Bob.

I wanted them to know that they could take pride in his special skills which impacted every one of them in some way. After sharing with them his background with the U.S. Air Force and his work with the FAA, I told them of the special relationship he had with their national airline and related to them the special honor afforded him by the captain of the Qantas flight.

Now for the clincher.

"Bob personally certified the pilot," I concluded with a moment of pride.

Their response to my statement?

They visibly leaned back in the pews as far as they could. A universal and identical frown appeared on the brow of every person in the congregation.

You do not have to be a genius to know when you have said the wrong thing. My problem was that I could not imagine how offense could be taken to what I thought was my perfect introduction.

Rev. John Taylor, wise beyond his years and my years, too, sensed my bewilderment.

He immediately seized the moment and observed that I

had just witnessed a classic example of American English as a foreign language in Australia.

"Here, Dr. Dawson, we use the term 'certify' when we swear in court that someone is insane."

He laughed; Bob laughed; the congregation laughed; I laughed (sort of).

Only in retrospect have I come to realize that what I said, and saw, and felt, is but a glimpse of the effect of our efforts to communicate daily with those people around us who speak "our language" but hear the wrong message.

How Much Fun
Can One Person Stand?

The Southern Baptist Convention has a penchant for stirring up vociferous debate over issues which "outsiders" find confusing, amazing, entertaining, or plain old dumb.

The problem for the Convention is that it is difficult to carry on an internal debate to the exclusion of the secular press in particular and the curious world in general.

A case in point was the debate that raged over the selection of Las Vegas as the site for the annual meeting of the Southern Baptist Convention. With decisions on such matters being made six or seven years in advance, it could hardly have been classified as a secret when the time came to have the big show.

The rhetoric grew so hot and the words got so descriptive that leaders began to fear that a genuine mission opportunity was about to be damaged beyond redemption by the animosity being generated by offended folks in the host city.

The image of self-appointed "good people" coming to subdue an evil environment did not do much to endear the image of Baptists as they arrived.

Amazingly enough, the folks at Las Vegas did not seem to

take Southern Baptists as seriously as we were prone to take ourselves.

When I arrived at the airport, I marched directly to the rental car outlets to claim my modest transportation needed to haul the materials the Christian Education Coordinating Board needed for its booth at the Convention Center.

> "Driving that car is probably the only fun you are going to have while you are in town!"

I was greeted warmly and sincerely by the attendant at the rental booth. I gave my name to claim my reservation and produced my driver's license and my credit card.

"Sir," she said. "I note that you are an employee of the Baptist General Convention of Texas and have reserved an economy class car for your use while you are in Vegas. I am going to take the liberty of upgrading your reservation at no cost to you. I am putting you in a full-size Buick."

As I tried to think of some appropriate words of appreciation, she provided me some added information.

"Driving that car is probably the only fun you are going to have while you are in town!"

In a town filled with the artificial and the fake, I was sort of "ticked off" when I saw the genuine twinkle in her eyes. To this day I have not been able to decide if I had been complimented or chided.

"Somebody Stole My Gal"

If you ask any seasoned traveler to show you the photo collection from his or her last trip to Europe, you will mostly likely end up admiring some very predictable shots.

Castles generally attract the greatest attention for the simple reason that they are not duplicated to any degree in the

United States. When I am invited to speak to public school classes about Europe, the teacher generally makes a special appeal for me to bring video presentations of our visits to an almost predictable list of castles.

Cathedrals rank up close to the top of the memory list, especially if the trip was part of a guided tour. No trip up or down the Rhine is complete without an awe-inspiring walk through the monumental Cologne cathedral. Besides that, they are easy to get to and are inexpensive.

But if the travelers were driving through Europe and free to do as they pleased, go where they wished, or spend as much time as it took to satisfy their curiosities, you will be treated to a special trip down their memory lane. You are introduced to their "memory makers."

It is while they are showing you those "special" pictures that they are most apt to pause and savor the moment being relived with you.

On a trip to Germany with Robert and Mary Lea Hefner, our friends asked what has come to be a routine request with friends with whom we travel.

"If we have time, could you show us your favorite 'memory maker?'"

Without hesitation we made immediate plans to take them to the monastery at Furstenfeldbruck, a short distance northwest of Munich.

People who judge and rank such things say that the chapels in the monasteries at Furstenfeldbruck and Ottobeuren are the two most beautiful examples of Baroque architecture in Germany. Each is the key component in an active "working" monastery, but only Ottobeuren is open for visitors on a daily basis except for worship periods. Furstenfeldbruck can be visited only between 10:00 A.M. and 11:00 A.M. on Friday. No exceptions!

Each is out of the way, in use, and without question worth the time and effort it takes to get there. The very limited window of opportunity at Furstenfeldbruck means that most travelers never get the opportunity to relish the moment of sitting outside the coffee shop across from the entrance to the monastery and counting the seconds before they can enter that incredible sanctuary.

The only feeling to rival the entrance is the moment of solitude at the same coffee shop after the 3,600-second experience in the beautiful Baroque chapel.

It was precisely at the moment I had chosen to take some footage of the scene and try to capture the essence of the visit that an almost incredible sound sort of drifted over us. All four of us heard the same sound and reacted with the same phrase.

"Is that Dixieland jazz?"

As we looked toward the monastery we could hear what could pass for the main attraction on Saturday night at Preservation Hall in New Orleans. The last thing I expected to hear was the sound of quality Dixieland Jazz pouring out the windows of the monk's quarters of a monastery in old Bavaria.

When we tried to find the exact source, it became evident that what we were hearing only seemed to come from the windows of the monastery. It was actually coming from around the corner and producing an echo effect off of the stone surface of the monastery wall.

In a small area around the corner was a tent filled with tables displaying arts and crafts. A large sign in front of the tent invited all to come, browse, and enjoy the music of Hot Lips Harry and his Munich Four (a rough translation from the German sign). Sales would benefit the good work of the monastery.

I must confess that the very last thing in this world I had expected was a Dixieland Jazz performance outside the monastery of Furstenfeldbruck. Actually it was the second most incredulous of my expectations.

Number one was when the band broke into a rendition of "Somebody Stole My Gal."

That sealed the experience in our memories forever.

It also gave rise to what seemed an appropriate pun:

"If it ain't Baroque, don't fix it!"

The Power of Concentration

Students of philosophy, theology, or the history of Germany are familiar with the name Friedrich Ernst Daniel Schleiermacher (1768-1834), who left a lasting imprint on history as a cofounder and lecturer at the University of Berlin and pastor of the Church of the Trinity in Berlin.

My general interest in Schleiermacher began with my undergraduate studies in German philosophy and, in particular, the Romanticists.

The topic of my MA thesis was the Young Hegelian movement. Schleiermacher was a large part of the story.

It was a natural development of that interest that led me to select the evolution of Schleiermacher's nationalism as the research topic for my doctoral studies and my dissertation which was ultimately published as *Friedrich Schleiermacher: The Evolution of a Nationalist* by the University of Texas Press.

One of Schleiermacher's qualities which constantly revitalized my interest in him was his capacity to maintain an incredible focus on tasks at hand.

A case in point: the battle for the city of Halle in 1806.

In a letter to his wife in 1806, Schleiermacher records in graphic detail how he became personally involved in the conflict for the city where he served on the faculty of the University of Halle.

He and a friend had watched the battle between French and Prussian troops for the bridge in the center of the city, but the French prevailed, and Schleiermacher eventually got caught between the two armies as the French advanced.

Schleiermacher explained to his wife that they somehow made it to his apartment and were hurriedly packing their belongings for flight when the French troops arrived.

He then describes in detail how the entire population of his building, more than thirty people, were herded by the French troops into his apartment. The sound of buildings being destroyed, and the smell of burning structures terrified the captives. This was made all the worse by three days of taunting and threats to set the apartment afire. The threats of violence were made all the worse by the execution of some of the domestic servants.

Schleiermacher closes his description of the chaos and horror that we call war with an assurance to his beloved.

"I have not let this interfere with my translation of Plato. It is coming along wonderfully well!"

During the most stressful week in his life, Schleiermacher completed a major portion of his translation of *Phaedrus* which is still considered one of the finer translations of this work from Greek to German.

There is nothing like tending to a little task when you have some idle time on your hands.

Faith Beyond the Grave

Friedrich Schleiermacher remained on focus his entire life with regard to the dream of a unified German nation.

After the French closed the University of Halle, Schleiermacher made his way to Berlin where he focused every thought and deed upon the unification of the German people and the liberation of Prussia from French occupation and oversight.

He served as a spy for his government and narrowly escaped discovery and imprisonment on several occasions. His speeches to his own students at the newly created University of Berlin led to a mass enrollment in volunteer fighting units that played decisive military roles in the War of Liberation.

After the end of the Napoleonic wars there was ushered into Europe an era which frowned upon the nationalistic expressions of men like Schleiermacher.

Throughout the period called the Age of Metternich, Schleiermacher continued through every available avenue and means of influence to work toward the day when his German people might be one nation.

By 1832, just months before his death, Schleiermacher finally came to the place where he despaired of ever seeing his dream of unification become a reality. In a letter to his wife he concluded that he now held little hope that he would ever see his high hopes realized.

He concluded that the only hope was that someday some strong person would emerge as a leader with the iron will to bring the various states of Germany together.

In an amazing demonstration of historical coincidence, after writing the letter he took a carriage ride to participate in the baptismal confirmation service for the young man who would become known as the Iron Chancellor, Otto von Bismarck, *the man credited with the unification of Germany.*

Who can know that a dream is lost? Sometimes we get to see the end of the dreaming and the beginning of the fulfillment all at the same time but never know which is taking place.

Inside the Castle

An interesting attribute of the medieval mindset which prevails on a typical college or university campus is the tendency to look upon the campus (castle) as a world of its own. What takes place there is judged by the standards of the castle and not the outside world.

Most of the time, the isolation of the campus from the "real" world is accepted by all as a natural and harmless circumstance. When the "real" world takes note of, and exception to, the medieval view of the world, the inhabitants behind the figurative walls often are at a loss to understand, much less explain, their complaints.

The insular nature of the campus is pervasive. The insular nature of a church-related institution is even more pronounced, due mainly to the addition of theology to the mix. Not every citizen feels the urge or the capability to address the ethics, or lack thereof, involved in an academic program. Every member of a denomination may feel the right, even the

DIVINE right, to address the theological position of the school which the denomination supports.

The key is to keep the discussion of theological questions within the hallowed walls of the institution. It is when the average person signs on to it at the level of the local church that really humorous, and sometimes, hilarious observations hit the press.

In recent years a major church-related university in Texas became the center of one of those issues that started with a simmer and almost immediately reached the boiling point.

The art department was accused of using nude drawings in one of their courses. (Surprise! Ever notice that no one ever takes exception to the choice of calculus textbooks?)

A letter or two here and there.

An inquiry or two, followed by a news article or two.

A sermon or two, followed by more of the first two.

Within a few days of the first public mention of the issue of the use of the textbook in the art class, the university was faced with a statewide assault by those "fur or agin it."

My office at the Baptist Building in Dallas got more calls from upset members of the denomination concerning this issue than any other issue in my decade of keeping track of such things.

Why?

The answer to that question can be found in the words of a pastor in the Golden Triangle.

He began his telephone conversation by saying that this was the first such call he had ever made in his life.

He described his church as one of the smallest in the county. It was the only church he had pastored, and he was the only pastor the church had ever had. Most members of the church had no other church experience.

As he put it, "What they know is what I have taught them."

He admitted that his folks did not have any theological training. They didn't know much about the millennium, the rapture, five point Calvinism, or dispensationalism.

"But they know *naked*," he asserted, "and they are against it!"

The Train is Waiting

I recently received an inquiry from a pastor search committee regarding the personal character of a preacher they were considering. Contrary to the current trend of looking into every theological nook and cranny of his life, this committee asked for only one bit of information.

"If you were to use one word to describe the life and ministry of this man, what would that one word be, and why?"

After playing word games for several days I finally responded to the letter with about the tenth version of my "one word" thesis. Then I found myself in the curious mode of trying to come up with single-word descriptions of friends, sermons, pets, newscasters, coaches, fat-free foods, and unsolicited telephone sales pitches after 6:00 P.M.

Mind you, asking any historian to describe anything in less than 500-year sweeps is wishful thinking when the use of terms like "circle the wagons" can bring differing descriptions if some of your ancestors were cowboys and some were Choctaws.

All of this is to say that I amazed even myself on a trip to Germany in 1997 on behalf of the Partnership Missions program of the Baptist General Convention of Texas. My first glimpse of this familiar terrain elicited the single word which for me personifies the composite picture of Germany—*Ordnung*.

No word says it better. The Germans are an orderly people. Clean, neat, fixed, painted, arranged, lined up, private, respectful, planned, organized. Everything in its place.

It also struck me that *Ordnung* is about as close as you can get to the perfect antithesis of Americans in general, Texans in particular, and **TEXAS BAPTISTS** in bold caps.

Not that there is anything wrong with a well-ordered society. If you took five times the population of Texas and crammed them all into Minnesota and Wisconsin, it would require orderliness. Texans love freedom and open spaces. Germans like order.

And here I was, visiting several churches affiliated with the German Baptist Union to explore potential areas where Texas Baptists might be able to assist German Baptists through a partnership agreement beginning January 1, 1999, and ending three years later.

We crossed Germany from Regensburg to Cloppenburg, Hannover to Hamburg, Brandenburg to Berlin. The more I renewed my appreciation for German culture and history, the more I became uncomfortably aware of the hills which remained to be climbed in order for the partnership to succeed.

Then came the trip by train from Berlin to Hildburghausen. Nothing personifies the German sense of order like their train system. The system works. The Father was about to use this wonderful example of precision to teach me the real meaning of *Ordnung*.

We boarded the train bound for Bavaria at Berlin with our schedule calling for us to pass through Erfurt and change trains at Grimmenthal for our ultimate destination, a small town with medieval roots—Hildburghausen.

As soon as the train slowed for track construction near Luther's Wittenburg, I began to get an uneasy feeling. In spite of the dependability of the German rail system, I knew we were not going to get to Grimmenthal in time to catch the last train to Hildburghausen.

Reconstruction of the antiquated East German rail system was about to do us in, and Steve Brubaker, SBC missionary to Germany, was going to await our arrival in vain.

At that point, enter Wolfgang Scholle.

Somehow the Lord arranged for us to share our compartment with this wonderful personality. He was obviously a man with a story—every German has one if you have the patience and the courtesy to inquire in an appropriate manner.

Herr Scholle had built a factory in East Germany after World War II, and it flourished until 1948, when the Communist regime decided that they needed it more than Herr Scholle did.

He and his brother made their way to Wiesbaden with forty-five Deutsche Mark and an undeniable determination to "start all over."

He said that the greatest moment in his life was in 1991 when he had made his way back to East Germany and used cash to buy back the factory which had been rightfully his. He instituted West German management techniques and turned the enterprise into a profitable business.

Herr Scholle hastened to add that he had determined from the outset to return all profits from the factory to help rebuild the small town around the factory. He said that his greatest gift to his former home was a vision for a better tomorrow and the rediscovery of a dream.

It was precisely at that point (in what had now been a one-hour discourse, some in German, some in English, some in funny little combinations of both), that I felt the boldness to interject my story into his.

I told him that I had come to Germany for the same reason he had returned to old East Germany. I represented Texas Baptist folks in general, and students in particular, who wanted to come to Germany to help German young people discover a new vision and dream a new dream for a better spiritual relationship with God.

"Gans gut! (wonderful). *Ausgezeichnet* (outstanding)," he exclaimed. "I like that."

Then he extended his hand, tears flowed, and we met on the common ground that God gives when people from different cultures meet at THE CROSS. He gave me his card, together with a promise of assistance to any request for help I might make.

I had no reason at that point to believe or not believe anything he had told me. Even his pledge to help did not mean that he could, or would, actually be of genuine assistance.

At this point I shared my worst fear. I told him that I was about to be a very embarrassed American and create a very bad first impression with our host and hostess in Hildburghausen.

The simple fact was that our train had only an eight minute window at Grimmenthal, and we were going to miss our connection. It was the last train out for the day, and there was no way for us to make our appointment.

His response?

"Das tut mir lied," he murmured. (Too bad, old buddy.)

Then, *"Ein Augenblick, bitte."* (Give me a moment, please.)

He left the compartment, returning in about five minutes with a smile and the most amazing announcement I have ever heard.

"They are holding the train for you at Grimmenthal," he said triumphantly.

Holding the train? A German train waiting for an American family? What about *Ordnung?*

> There is a great likelihood that somewhere, somebody is waiting for you to give them a new hope for today and a faith in tomorrow. But they may not hold the train forever.

Sure enough, when we got off the train at Grimmenthal and waved a hearty farewell to Wolfgang Scholle, we saw an amazing sight. The conductor and his assistant were making their way to us. It may be the only time in my life, or my life hereafter, that a German train conductor carries my luggage. He was kind enough not to mention that he was now twenty-eight minutes late.

Margie felt a touch of concern as we neared the train, walking as closely as possible behind the conductor and his associate. "I'll bet the folks on that train are really mad at us for holding up their train," she almost whispered to me.

"Are you kidding? My guess is that they are scared to death of us," I quickly replied.

It took a few minutes on board the train for me to come to an obvious conclusion. I had been fretting about free-wheeling Texans joining with orderly Germans in a novel experiment in cooperation. How would we ever find a common ground on which to build our efforts?

Then I had been treated to a demonstration by the Father of *Ordnung.*

It sure makes one wonder where they may be holding a train for *you,* doesn't it?

There is a great likelihood that somewhere, somebody is waiting for you to give them a new hope for today and a faith in tomorrow. But they may not hold the train forever.

The Train Waited, Thank Goodness

The train ride from Grimmenthal to Hildburghausen was especially satisfying. The chances were astronomically slim that I would ever be treated so royally again.

I could not help but call to Margie's attention that while this might be my last opportunity to catch a waiting train, it was not my first. Once before, in 1939, I had had a somewhat similar experience.

Our family lived in what we always called "the green house." We called it that because it was painted green. In Borger, Texas, and particularly on East Fourth and Whittenburg Street in Borger, everything else was black.

What managed to go unsoiled by the half-circle of carbon black plants around the town and smoke from the burn pit of an oil well one block from the house was finished off by soot from trains on the track which ran almost directly behind our house.

Soot and noise were not the only byproducts of the train. The rail yards, which began south of East Third Street, were at the end of the track. Trains did not come "through" Borger, only "to" Borger. Many a hobo unwittingly caught a ride out of Amarillo only to discover he had made a bad mistake. Our house was on the hobo trail that led away from the tracks.

For all of the reasons above, the constant admonition from mothers in the neighborhood was "stay off of the tracks." And for all of the same reasons, the constant challenge to kids in the neighborhood was to confront the trains as the enemy.

It takes collective genius to come up with a scheme to deal

misery to a train. Various meetings with D-Boy and O-Boy Miller, Rex Haley, and Willis Ray Ging gave ample opportunity to concoct a scheme, but always our ideas were the kind of kid stuff that lay well beyond the realm of possibility.

Beyond the realm, that is, until a short cartoon found its way into the Saturday morning show at of the Crown Theater. Some ingenious kids decided to flag down a train to save a hero.

Bingo! Flag down a train!

Rex, Willis Ray, and yours truly walked the five blocks from the Crown Theater to the tracks and waited for a train to "make up" in the yards.

As soon as the engineer moved to the Pampa highway and eased northward toward Phillips with his load of empty tank cars, we got up on the tracks and waved our arms in the air.

It was not much of a train. I remember that part pretty clearly.

It wasn't much fun, either.

The engineer had the bad manners to blow his whistle.

Three mothers had the bad manners to respond.

My own sweet mother, who was prone to use mesquite branches, helped me find my way to the house with loving nudges to my posterior.

I never could figure what people got out of messing with trains after that.

At least the Germans carried my luggage and smiled.

Two trains in one lifetime seems like a pretty good showing.

Only Place in Town

Volunteerism is the driving energy of American life.

Sometime in their life most folks will focus their time, emotions, energy, and sense of commitment on behalf of some issue or cause which elicits their best efforts without any accompanying promise of personal gain.

For me, the threat to American society posed by the use of drugs in the era of the 1960s seemed worthy of my time. Texas Alcohol Narcotics Education, Inc. (TANE) caught both my attention and my spirit of volunteerism.

I became part of, and eventually head of, the speaker's bureau for TANE at Wayland Baptist College. Some of my fondest memories relate to Sunday morning trips to distant, remote churches spread across the Texas Panhandle and South Plains with carloads of speakers willing to give of their time and talents to awaken a sense of urgency about the drug problem.

Some "less than fond" memories also registered in my memory bank on these trips. And most of these came as a result of trying to find a place to eat lunch.

One particularly "memorable" trip started about 7:00 A.M. in Plainview and led to Estelline, Childress, Lakeview, and Leslie. By the time I had completed services and gathered up Bennie Wright, Billy Yell, Tom Cole, and Wayman Culp, it was nearly 2:00 P.M., and hunger was running amuck in the car.

If there is any town in Texas where hunger ought not run amuck on Sunday afternoon, that town is Turkey.

It may be that Turkey's greatest claim to fame is the fact that it was the hometown of Bob Wills, the founder of one of the more famous Western musical bands in Texas. But you know you are in trouble when you want to eat in Turkey instead of dancing.

By the very simple process of elimination, our search led us to a little café located where main street dead-ended into a farm-to-market trail. The café's sole asset seemed to be its availability. It did not speak well for them that we were the only customers.

The waitress was apparently a veteran of lonely Sunday campaigns. She walked to our table, took out her order pad, and said, "Okay."

To which I responded, "Might we see a menu?"

"Don't need one," she said with a strong sense of closure. "All we have is chicken fried steak and hamburgers."

"Are the steaks good?" I inquired in an effort to interject a little humor into what seemed like a pretty hopeless situation.

"Doesn't make any difference," she asserted with an air of triumph. "We're the only place in town!"

Suddenly I felt like I was back in church.

Wooden Legs and Warm Hearts

When I started my collegiate career at Wayland Baptist College in 1952, one of the first acquaintances I made was a fellow named Bob.

Like me, he had a background rooted in the oil fields. He was a welder, and both my father and my father-in-law were welders. He was working his way through school, trying his best to raise a family, and all the while sought to know clearly the call of God in his life.

Eight years after I transferred from Wayland to Mississippi College to pursue a major in philosophy, I had the happy privilege of returning to Wayland as an assistant professor of history.

Soon thereafter, when we placed our membership in College Heights Baptist Church, we were blessed with the opportunity to renew our friendship and fellowship with Bob and his family.

Only then did I come to understand the strange turn Bob's life had taken. He had suffered the loss of one leg when a pipe rolled over him. School, studies, and preparation for the ministry had all been placed on hold as Bob and his family faced the difficult and personally demanding task of coping with an artificial leg, and the vast medical expenses that went with it.

Bob never lost a glimmer of his hope for special service in the Kingdom's work, but he often seemed at a loss to understand and find meaning in the loss of his leg, and the resulting "hold" it had placed on his life.

Never once did he express any feeling except gratitude that someday he would understand what had taken place.

Then came a news broadcast that electrified the entire city of Plainview.

A local high school football hero had had a tragic accident on one of the many playa lakes that surround Plainview. These lakes are common in the flat terrain of the Staked Plains, but they are also temporary. Spring rains form these lakes, and they last until summer evaporation reclaims the lake beds.

What appears to be a lake fit for water-skiing often is a dangerously shallow bed of water covering all kinds of debris immediately below the surface.

Several young high school athletes found to their sorrow that the debris in their playa lake would cost one of them his leg.

The news accounts added a chilling commentary about the accident. The loss of his limb, and the end of his football career, and the loss of hope that often accompanies such tragedies, had thrown the young athlete into a terrible and profound depression.

"Street" talk added a last word to the already somber story. Our young hero was staring into a void. He would not respond to any stimuli or to anyone's presence. Unless something could be done to break the state of depression, there was reason to fear for life itself.

It was then that Bob was galvanized into action.

He went to the hospital and volunteered his services. His plan was bold but simple. He went to the hospital room of a person he understood as no one else in Plainview understood. He sat on the foot of the bed, facing his fellow sufferer.

No response.

Then he reached down and elevated his wooden leg so that it was next to the "good" leg of his fellow sufferer.

No response.

Then he reached into his pocket and took out his pocket knife and opened the big blade.

No response.

Then Bob deliberately began to play mumble peg with his wooden foot which was positioned only inches from the heart of his fellow sufferer.

One throw. The blade buried in the artificial foot.

No response.

Two throws. Again the blade buried in the foot.

Again, no response.

Finally, after several additional throws, A GLANCE!

When he was sure that he had won a hearing, Bob said, "You know, there is not one person in a million that can do this to their foot."

Then their eyes met. Hope was born when the despairing athlete realized that someone "really understood" his loss.

Later, after life was reclaimed and heroics were a more common part of their lives, Bob admitted that it might just be so that the loss of his own leg had placed him in the unique roll of fellow sufferer with one in need.

That should not come as a surprise. The Father assures us that He more than understands every depressing aspect of our life. He knows the difference between leaving a tragedy and entering a miracle.

Three People, Two Prayers, One Answer

Randy was the gentle one.

Of all our children (three), grandchildren (eight), nieces and nephews (multitudes), Randy was the one whom all of the others treated with a special sense of kindness in response to his own natural display of affection.

He was the friend among a lot of people who had small or very carefully selected circles of associates they called friends.

He was a giving person. It never seemed to dawn upon him that he should be the recipient of anything from anyone.

All of this became evident at his funeral services.

One minute Randy was riding with friends in slow moving traffic on Sunday afternoon, and the next minute he was called Home.

As the literal multitudes made their way to the funeral home to pay their respects to the family for the thirty-six years of Randy's life and influence, one was struck by the incredible diversity of types, ages, personalities, and careers of those who came.

All agreed that Randy himself would have been amazed at the effect his life had had on so many people in so many ways for so many days.

Penny and Elzie somehow made it through the numbing maze that comes with losing a grown son by a sudden accident. But finally the flowers were all given, the kinfolks went home, the house was closed, and special considerations were given to his personal belongings for the sake of remembrances.

It seems that each day became a little more bearable and each decision a little less heart-rending.

Then came a call that seemed to bring everything back.

There was a question about liability, or was it responsibility? Or perhaps accountability?

This was something Penny and Elzie could only face together, but alone. Penny saw the car drive up, and she turned to Elzie with a plea for prayer that they might make it through this terrible moment with the help of a loving God. In particular they prayed that the man who was to speak to them would be gentle and loving.

They finished their prayer and then noticed that their visitor was still seated in his automobile. He had not stirred for a quarter of an hour.

When he came to the door, their visitor seemed shaken. He confided with Penny and Elzie that he was new at his task and was sorry that he had kept them waiting. He had been overcome with a great need to pray when he arrived. He hoped that his prayer time had not kept them waiting.

When asked about the object of his prayers, he confessed that he had asked the Father to make him kind and gentle in his visit with them.

The time together revealed to the three of them that Randy had indeed been as kind, considerate, and giving toward his parents in his death as they had been toward him in his life.

At the very least, this is but a glimpse of the provisions made for us by the Father.

It will be a surprise to all of us.

Watch Out

There has always been a mystique about a person's "last words."

In an argument, the desire to get in the "last word" often creates the most lasting pain.

In court cases, the last word often determines the decision concerning the guilt or innocence of a defendant.

In church services, the promise of "last words" by the pastor often requires faith, which is by definition the substance of things hoped for, the evidence of things not seen.

The "last words" most fraught with peril in travel are the words, "Is there anything we can get for you while we are there?"

I very casually asked this of my daughter Jamie as Margie and I prepared to get on our flight to Frankfurt.

Big mistake!

Without a blink she said that she had always wanted a nice Swiss watch.

Gulp!

Trying to cover the emerging pain of premature death in my billfold, I nonchalantly asked if just any old Swiss watch would do, or did she have something special in mind?

Mistaking the pale face and shaking hands for pre-flight anxiety, Jamie rushed to my aid with a precise definition of her heart's desire.

"A heart-shaped watch would thrill me to death," she answered.

As we turned for the boarding gate I sensed that "death" seemed an appropriate designation for what I had gotten myself into with my "last words."

For a good portion of our trip fate spared me the agony of having to complete Jamie's eternal quest for a heart-shaped watch. No one seemed to have the faintest notion as to a likely source. Then came a famous shop in Lucerne and a watch that even I had to admit was precisely what our daughter wanted, and deserved.

The watch became the object of a lot of attention for several months, and then it died.

Come to find out, getting the watch had been a piece of cake. Getting it running again became a nightmare.

No matter where we took the watch, we got the same reception.

"We don't work on that brand of watch. You will have to get the seller to honor the warranty on it."

After a while it became obvious that no one in the Metroplex had the slightest interest in attempting to repair my sweetheart's heart-shaped watch.

The last thing I wanted to do was to ship the watch off to Europe, just hoping that I would somehow get it returned and win back the confidence that my daughter had in her dad's ability to get things done.

Almost by chance, I had to make a very quick trip to Europe and would pass through Zurich on the train. I had an hour between trains, and it just happened that there was in Zurich a branch of the Lucerne business where I bought the watch.

My plan was simple. Get off the train in Zurich, dash up the Bahnhofstrasse to the store, leave the watch, run back to the station, and then head for Interlaken. The next day I would reverse the trail, all the while hoping that the watch would be ready.

The whole plan went off without a hitch, and I was actually feeling a sense of James Bondness the second day when I arrived precisely on my pre-determined schedule at the counter. The watch-master was waiting with said watch in hand. When he saw my flushed face and trickling perspiration, he seemed moved by my personal commitment to detail and planning.

He complimented me for devoting precious travel time and

> It is a lot like trying to have a meaningful relationship with the Heavenly Father. We are the ones who complicate the process.

energy to make sure personally that my daughter's concerns were attended to.

"After all," he said, "all it needed was a battery. You can get them at your Kmart."

All the way back to Texas I pondered the mystery of how I could turn something so simple into such a complex and personally demanding ordeal.

It is a lot like trying to have a meaningful relationship with the Heavenly Father. We are the ones who complicate the process.

Pure Hearts and Red Snow

A word of warning should always be personally delivered and signed for by each and every person who decides to volunteer for mission trips outside the U.S.A. That warning should read:

Beware!

You are about to enter into a
process that is destined to change
your spiritual perspective forever.

Margie and I joined hands with Bill Gray and the Office of Texas Baptist Partnership Missions in 1994 in an effort to help Estonian Baptists complete the building of their new seminary in Tartu.

Estonian Baptists, numbering less than one hundred congregations after the end of the brutal occupation by the Soviet Union in 1991, emerged from the shadows of illegal existence and set as one of their first goals the building of a theological seminary.

Thanks to the aid of Baptists from all over the world, the project was undertaken. Three years later it was nearing completion thanks to unbelievable construction efforts by churches like the First Baptist Church of Bryan, Texas.

I thought the purpose of the trip was to figure out ways to help these valiant folks complete their project and create a link with the Texas Baptist Division of Student Work.

I soon learned that the Father had arranged for my presence so that I might experience firsthand the incredible courage of people who suffered beyond description for their devotion to the name of Jesus.

I remember, for obvious reasons, the prayer by one of our hosts at our first luncheon in Estonia. He said, "Lord, we thank thee that we do not have to go into the woods to voice this prayer."

It seems like we were moved by the story of every Christian we met. After all, to survive the Communist regime was in itself a story filled with valor and commitment.

Tonu Lehtsaar was one of those remarkable personalities who managed to hold on to his grasp of God's hand and with his nation emerge from the past with an eagerness to get on with life without rancor or hatred.

> "Lord, we thank thee that we do not have to go into the woods to voice this prayer."

His academic accomplishments were impressive. He had published research in five languages and had conversational skills in four more. He pastored in the Tartu area, taught at the Estonian seminary meeting in temporary quarters at Calvary Baptist Church, was a member of the faculty of the University of Tartu, and held key leadership positions in the Evangelical Union of Estonia.

Subsequent to our visit, Tonu accepted a one-year appointment as a visiting professor of Missions at Southwestern Baptist Theological Seminary in Fort Worth, Texas. While there, Tonu was given a special hearing by the graduate dean and the administrative council of Baylor University. This evaluation resulted in the unprecedented offer to allow Professor Lehtsaar to complete doctoral residence requirements in a single year.

When Dean Walbesser was questioned regarding this remarkable departure from administrative practice at Baylor,

Dr. Walbesser said that many of the members of the reviewing group were moved by the vision of this man.

He confessed that Dr. Lehtsaar "is the first person I have ever met who felt that he could help win his entire country for the cause of Christ."

Unfortunately, the call to return to Estonia superseded his wishes to stay in Texas.

When Tonu, or his lovely wife Tati, spoke, I had the understandable urge to listen *very* carefully. My most treasured memory of his many reminiscences came about when the family visited our home at Christmas time.

Tonu said his father had suffered under the Communists both for his faith and for his guilt by association with people of the faith.

He served his church in Tartu as a volunteer janitor. It did not take long after the imposition of Communist oppression for him to draw the attention and disfavor of the ruling regime.

He was sent to Siberia and endured indescribable misery in return for his determination to make presentable his house of worship.

After the death of Joseph Stalin many prisoners were inexplicably allowed to find their way home "on their own." This added element of oppression caused a three-year delay, but eventually Mr. Lehtsaar returned to Tartu and tried to put the pieces of a shattered life back together.

Marriage and children helped replace the memories of the camps with a new hope for a better life, though the yoke of Communism remained seemingly permanent until the breakup of the Soviet system began in earnest in 1991.

The breath of fresh air that came with the departure of Communist controls by 1991 opened a brief crack in the wall that Mr. Lehtsaar had built to seal off the terrible memories of his suffering.

Tonu said that his father had never once spoken of the days in Siberia until a memorable morning in January on their way to church.

It was crystal clear and incredibly cold as the family walked toward church. Father Lehtsaar turned to Tonu and Tati and said, "What a beautiful day. This reminds me of a day when we were walking to the mines in Siberia."

Tonu said that they were astonished by this unprecedented reference to his gruesome past. But before anyone could muster appropriate words of response, he added, "Of course, it was different. The snow was red."

Tonu casually inquired as to the source of the color.

To this, his father responded, "Oh, from the blood. You see, we had no shoes."

The incredible part of Tonu's account was that his father remembered the day as one of beauty.

I pray that I am never required to leave my blood on a snowy trail because I dared to volunteer to sweep the floors of my Heavenly Father's house. If it ever comes to that, I pray that I will remember that Jesus was willing to leave a trail of his blood so that my life, the Temple of the Holy Spirit, might be made clean.

The Samson Syndrome

The Bible is filled with personalities whose lives and ministries are worthy role models for our contemporary society.

- Paul and his missionary zeal

- Moses and his incredible qualities of leadership
- Peter and his profoundly simple faith
- David and his Psalmist visions of godliness
- Isaiah and his prophetic vision

But one Biblical character who has always attracted almost universal interest is Samson.

Everything about him was unusual. His weapons of war with the enemies of Israel included such an unlikely device as the jawbone of a donkey. Among his object lessons to his enemies included the theft of the gates to the chief walled city of the Philistines. He died by destroying the very foundations of the temple of his enemies and lost his own life in the process.

The thread which runs through the fabric of all of the accounts of his deeds is that of his physical strength. And therein lies his chief appeal. Every person, every church, every city, every high school football team, some time and in some way, gets caught up by the desire to excel, win it all, be the best, win the greatest victory. Someone has called it the Samson Syndrome.

I got a perfect personal introduction to this attraction with my own sons when they were five and four.

The makers of Meal-O-Malt (the name has been changed to protect the innocent) were conducting a national advertising campaign which included a cartoon picturing two boys literally attacking a bowl of their product.

After licking the bowls clean, the two boys stepped to a nearby tree and pulled up the tree, roots and all, with one mighty tug.

From that very moment Kim and Carey began a personal campaign to get Margie to buy them a box of Meal-O-Malt. She knew, I knew, the world should have known that these two little guys were NOT ever going to develop a liking for Meal-O-Malt. (To this day it strikes me as pretty bad stuff.)

They were unrelenting. Every trip to the food store was highlighted by a dramatic appeal for mom to buy the "you know what."

On a hot July afternoon Margie finally succumbed to the sheer weight of numbers (two little fellows always outnumber one grown mother) and bought what she was fully convinced was to be a one-time purchase of Meal-O-Malt.

When they got back to the pastorium at McDade in the sweltering heat of a typical, Central Texas, July afternoon, nothing would do but that she should immediately cook a serving of what had become an obsession to our boys.

To their credit, they ate every bite of this awful brew without a single whimper. Gone! Vanished!

Then Kim looked over to his younger brother and said, "Come on, Carey. Let's go out and PULL UP A TREE!"

Who knows? They might have been able to pull up a tree. So might we all.

Come to think of it, all of us have a few trees that could stand a little tug or two. If we are given the directions for moving mountains, trees should be a cinch.

Called Or Sent?

One of the great experiences of my educational career was a doctoral seminar with Walter Prescott Webb at the University of Texas. Probably the most celebrated student of the role of the West in shaping the American experience, Webb dedicated the entire seminar to the effect of religious and social institutions upon the West in general and Texas in particular.

Allowing the free flow of ideas was a Webb hallmark. Not surprisingly, several members of the seminar chose to study the impact of the West upon religious denominations, and the corresponding impact of religious denominations upon the West.

Ground rules removed theology from the equation as the seminar sought to determine the relative success or failure of various denominations. For example, a Presbyterian minister in the class entitled his paper, "The West Says No to John Knox."

The composite conclusion reached by the class was that

Baptists seemed to have been the most successful in Texas. Why? The class concluded that the West responded most readily to a sense of "calling" rather than to a program of "sending." The individuality of Western life seemed compatible to individual response.

Since I was obviously a member of the hostile band of Baptist believers in their midst, Dr. Webb asked me to give the seminar what I considered to be the worst example I could think of with reference to the sense of "call."

Unwittingly, I gave him the best example instead.

I started my collegiate experience at Wayland Baptist College in Plainview, Texas, in September of 1952. As a young "preacher boy" I noticed that I was listed among more than one hundred who had felt the call to preach. With less than five hundred resident students, I was part of a very sizable minority.

I was also a member of a small minority within that band of "preacher boys." Having grown up in a home where there was no religious training, and having been converted at high school age, I was woefully short of the acquired skills so many of my classmates seemed to treasure.

And since my dad had worked for several years as floor bouncer at what most folks referred to as a honky-tonk, and my mother sold beverages there from time to time, I had already seen up close a lot of what my fellow ministers had never seen but universally decried.

In an effort to help us in clarifying our personal commitment to righteousness, Wayland required all students to sign a pledge not to drink, smoke, dance, or "anything" while enrolled at the school.

Whether by virtue of experience, or by the process of pure speculation, most of our "holy" students had arrived at a commonly accepted definition of appropriate behavior in the light of our "call" to the ministry.

About the only thing in common among the more than one hundred preachers-to-be was their belief that Grady Nutt was never going to make it.

No talent?

Goodness no. He could sing, preach, grin, think, or whatever.

His problem was that he was not serious.

Grady thought that this world was an incredibly funny place and that people were the funniest part of the whole universe. He even thought God was subject to a touch of humor now and then. And every preacher in the student body had already made a career of being serious.

Did I say serious?

I mean Serious.

No. I mean *SERIOUS*.

And the more serious the ministerial clan became, the more Grady Nutt rattled their devotional bird cage.

Just to hear Grady say "GAWWD" was an experience in blasphemy.

Grady later said that he was called into the office of Dean Bryan Robinson at the end of his first full semester and reminded that he had signed a pledge not to drink, smoke, dance, or "anything" while he was at Wayland.

Surprised, Grady assured him that he had not.

Allegedly, Dean Robinson replied, "No, but you wanted to!"

Everyone was sure of one simple but indisputable fact. Grady Nutt was never going to amount to anything unless he got serious—-called to the ministry or not!

Five years later in the Walter Prescott Webb seminar at the University of Texas, Grady still struck me as a classic example of the untrustworthiness of a sense of call as a test for the ministry. I could hardly imagine any random group of his peers sitting as an ordaining council and agreeing to ordain him to the ministry. The Grady Nutt I knew would never have been "sent."

Slightly more than two decades later I had the unique privilege of talking with Grady Nutt at a special outdoors evangelistic service at East Texas Baptist College. I watched and listened as Grady helped his student congregation laugh their way clear through the story of the prodigal son, and then cry their way through an invitation to "get serious about Jesus."

Grady Nutt was acclaimed at that time as the leading Christian humorist in America.

And I am pretty sure there were still those who were waiting for him to "get serious" so that he might "amount to something."

It certainly seemed a tragic turn of circumstances when his plane crashed a few weeks later near Texarkana.

Grady Nutt's story does give pause to the process of determining whether we are "sent" by them or called by Him.

Lock the Door

Most of my efforts aimed at bringing about change in the political landscape of Texas have been in the form of the ballot. Occasionally I have participated in petitions. On rare occasions when a sense of urgency seemed to demand my immediate input I have enlisted "Ma Bell" to deliver my message. Most of the time I have chosen the avenue of direct appeal, "face to face."

Once, and only once, have I felt compelled to make a serious request of a political figure after the results of an election had become final.

When Governor Bill Clements was sworn into the office of chief executive for the State of Texas, I became burdened with the need to share with him the key to reforming the entire political structure of our state government.

Repeated visits to Austin to speak to legislators, committees, panels, lobbyists, and secretaries had brought me to the conviction that there were incredibly large numbers of people who could be omitted from the whole process without affecting the course of good government.

My convictions jelled into a plan so daring and bold that I felt only a man of the stature of Bill Clements would have the fortitude to bring it to pass.

One week after his inauguration, I sent my plan to the governor's office.

The plan?

It was so simple.

Governor Clements should get a locksmith and proceed directly down each hall, corridor, nook, and cranny in each and every building owned, leased, rented, or borrowed for the use of state government. At every fifth door they should order all inhabitants out of the office and lock the door.

It would take weeks for most of the state to even notice that the doors were locked. Summer would come and go before some of the appointed people ever tried to open their door.

Really important work of government would be passed on to the next open door, but there was nothing new about that.

When people began to ask why their door was locked, and surely some would eventually do that, it would provide a wonderful opportunity to get an accurate accounting of the state payroll.

To function properly, the plan required only that it be executed relentlessly without regard to friend, foe, or figment of the imagination.

Was this not a great and profoundly simple solution to government growth run amuck?

I closed by saying that I felt that the vote I had cast for Bill Clements allowed me the privilege of suggesting this singular effort at governmental reform.

Three weeks later I received a letter from the office of Governor Bill Clements.

The letter stated that the office was taking this means to assure me that my request for consideration for appointment to service under the administration of the governor would be placed in an appropriate file. I should receive further communications concerning any appointment at a later date.

Good grief!

Show Me a Mesquite Tree

When I was growing up in Borger, Texas, I came to realize that rivers and trees were two things you read about in books or saw in movies, but they were outside the circles of strong influences in my life.

I can still remember going to Amarillo about 1940 and seeing the trees in the park near the Santa Fe Building. They were big! Trees were not big in Borger. I and Borger were born at almost the same time, and I was almost as old as the trees there, and just about as tall.

Actually, Borger was surrounded by trees. There were a couple over toward Pampa, and some say there was one past the Gulf camp toward Panhandle, and there were even totally unreliable accounts of tree sightings near the unpaved highway through Fritch toward Amarillo.

The few trees that were there were the sources for a special set of problems.

I still remember the beginning of my freshman year in Borger High School. My English teacher was Mrs. Brezny, a recent transplant from Chicago. I distinctly remember her saying that she had never been outside of Chicago until she came to Borger.

Mrs. Brezny was absolutely thrilled to see the West at last and be able to place in context the great literary treasures she had read since her youth.

Mrs. Brezny did not have to wait very long. The first story in our literature text was a classic by J. Frank Dobie. One of the pivotal scenes pictured several riders who were sitting on their horses in the shade of some mesquite trees.

SHOW AND TELL TIME at Borger High School.

Our teacher beamed with excitement.

"What is a mesquite tree?" she asked. "I have always pictured this scene in my mind, but I have never been able to make it come to life because I have yet to see one."

Not knowing any better than to volunteer, I asked, "Would you really like to see a mesquite tree?"

I walked briskly to her desk, took her by the hand, and led her to the window. There I discovered that I was really in luck. Not ten feet from the window stood a mesquite tree. All eight feet of it. Every scrawny branch of it. Seemed kind of strange that a Yankee school teacher would get excited about a bush like that.

I pointed to the mesquite and said in my most casual freshman tone, "There it is."

Mrs. Brezny's reaction to my declaration was to look desperately for a tree while she asked, "Where? All I see is that bush."

When she looked at me, I had the terrible feeling that she was very, very disappointed in my mesquite tree. I also got a sneaking premonition that she was going to hold me directly responsible for shattering her moment.

"I'm sorry, but that really is a mesquite tree," I told her.

When several of my classmates sensed my predicament, they assured their teacher that I had in fact pointed out to her a genuine mesquite tree.

We told her about a lot of things as the year progressed.

We reported sightings of jackrabbits that were five feet tall.

Some in the class swore to accounts of rattlesnakes that had eaten fully grown horses.

One student promised to bring to class a picture depicting prairie dogs in the very act of herding cattle.

And how about mockingbirds that could actually sing "The Eyes of Texas"?

Mrs. Brezny always believed that Dobie's mesquite trees were just another Western fantasy.

The fact that Dobie's stories were set hundreds of miles south of Borger never removed the moment of disillusionment that she had experienced that day in September.

And to this day I have been impressed by the staying power of a single moment of disillusionment. Almost everyone I know has had to deal with a fractured dream.

It is one thing to experience disillusionment when a tree fails to meet our expectations. It is infinitely worse to lose our faith in people.

Backing Off the Bridge

Only a Texan would refer to the Canadian River as a river. Cutting across the Texas Panhandle from west to east, it is like the statement a rancher's wife used to describe her husband when she said, "He ain't much, but he's all I got."

You can travel four hundred miles due south from the Canadian in the middle of the Panhandle and not cross running water. As a matter of fact, there have been times when you could cross the Canadian River and not cross running water.

Seventeen inches of annual rainfall does not form the source for impressive rivers. The fact that there was a river there "once in a while" formed the backdrop for one of those interesting little "slices of life" that define many of our days.

The Canadian River bridge a few miles north of Borger had several distinctive characteristics.

Counting the approaches and the structure, the bridge was about a mile long.

It was the only bridge across the Canadian for miles upstream or down.

It was a very narrow structure with very low clearance on top.

Worst of all, the spans were not uniform in height. The last span on the north end of the bridge had about six inches less clearance than the rest of the bridge.

I worked for J. M. Huber Corporation in the summer of 1952. Huber had oil and gas production on both sides of the Canadian, and our gang had been assigned the task of repairing a pipeline leak on the north side.

When we got to the southern approach to the bridge everything stopped.

It was the middle of the wheat harvest, and a truck loaded with two tractors and pulling a combine had started across the bridge with only inches of clearance at the top. The truck did just fine until the last span.

CRUNCH!

There was nothing to do but back the combine and truck for almost a mile. And before the truck could start the ordeal, every other vehicle had to back off.

It took almost half a day. We were standing on the first shoulder south of the bridge when the exhausted trucker climbed down from his rig. He was wringing wet from perspiration and trying his best to ignore the angry stares from the hundred or so irate drivers whose schedules had been altered.

When a reporter from Radio Station KHUZ asked him for a comment, he replied with all the wisdom of the ages of human experience.

"Getting on that bridge was not much. Getting off was SOMETHING ELSE."

A few days later, we noticed a hand-painted sign mounted on the guard rails next to the entrance to the bridge. "BRIDGES SHOULD BE JUDGED BY THEIR LOWEST SPAN."

There was not a person in the small audience at the south approach to the bridge that had not had the same experience in a different suit of clothes.

The list is endless and includes everything from immoral behavior to flawed church building projects.

The Scriptures say it well.

"There is a way that seemeth good to man, but the end thereof are the ways of death."

First Love

I have felt a commitment to ministry since 1952 at the end of my senior year in Borger High School.

And while I felt a "call" to ministry, I did not necessarily feel called to "the" ministry.

My freshman year at Wayland Baptist College helped me define the meaning of the sense of call, and I set my course for a career in Christian education. I transferred from Wayland to Mississippi College in 1954 so that I could prepare for an academic career that included majors in philosophy, history, and English.

One of my professors at MC recommended me to a wonderful little church in East Central Mississippi, Stratton Baptist Church. Though I explained to them that I was neither prepared nor qualified to pastor any church, even a "half-time" church with seventeen resident members, they called me as their pastor.

It was my first love affair with a church.

During my stay in Mississippi I had the privilege of trying to serve two additional half-time churches, but Stratton occupied that special place in my heart.

Upon completion of my undergraduate studies, I was granted a teaching fellowship in philosophy at the University of Texas at Austin.

Shortly after arriving in Austin in 1956, I received an invitation to preach at First Baptist Church in McDade. After several Sunday services together, and in spite of my protestations that I was preparing for an academic career at the collegiate level, the kind folks there called me as their pastor.

Thus began my second "first love" with a church. It was my one and only full-time church. It was four years of sweet fellowship, wonderful people, some progress, and our third child, Jamie.

Although I was forthright in telling the congregation that I was going to be a full-time student at the university, they responded as a healthy congregation by always encouraging me to press toward my goals.

While serving at McDade we became aware of the needs of a sister church a few miles away, Knobbs Springs Baptist Church. A pretty little church with a long and cherished past had declined to the point where it seemed to be faced with the necessity to close its doors. I had the happy privilege of assisting with efforts to bring the congregation back to life.

Thus was born another type of "first love" for a church.

When I completed my residency for my doctorate in European Intellectual History at the University of Texas in May of 1960, I accepted an appointment to the history faculty of Wayland Baptist College, my academic "first love."

The next spring I commenced a brand new phase of ministry within "the ministry."

I accepted the invitation to become interim pastor of First Baptist Church of Silverton, Texas. Thus began a new "first love." At this writing the interim pastorates number more than sixty, but Silverton will always have a special place in our heart. This is where I learned one of the great lessons of church life.

Silverton was a ranching community to the south and east of Palo Duro Canyon. From the first day I visited there, I was struck by the stark and hard existence that had confronted the early settlers. Many of the older people were first-generation occupants of their ranches and farms.

Mr. and Mrs. Doug Arnold were two of those hearty, tough, deep, and absolutely trustworthy pillars of their church. Every conversation with them was a learning experience for me.

One "front porch" session included a bit of discussion about the delicate item of age. I was struck by the fact that there seemed to be an inordinate number of women in the church in their late "eighties" or early "nineties."

It struck me that so many could reach that age in an environment which included cistern water, few doctors, harsh winters, blistering summers, long hours, hard work, prairie fires, and an adversarial soil.

Without realizing it, I was enumerating the excuses for human failure.

Mrs. Arnold's answer was wise.

"Dr. Dawson, there is an explanation for that. The weak ones all died young."

Would You Recognize Him?

Anon Card is one of those classic examples of a country boy who "done good."

A product of rural East Texas in general and Lufkin in particular, he relied upon his skills as a football player to open college doors that seemingly had been closed by the great depression.

Anon's first trip to the College of Marshall (now East Texas Baptist University) opened the world to his abilities and talents. Four decades later Anon and Fran returned to his alma mater to share with the graduating class some of the rich experiences of his fabled life which eventually had led to the presidency of Texaco in Houston, Texas.

It would be difficult to overstate the impact of his "common touch" upon the faculty, parents, seniors, and guests. It would be even more difficult to overstate the impression Anon and Fran made upon Jerry and Margie Dawson. They personified all of the end results which can accrue to those who follow their dream (and sweat a lot).

Before our guests left for home in Houston, the Cards extended to the Dawsons an invitation to "come see us sometime."

I mentioned that I might be able to work that into my busy schedule.

He responded by saying that he figured I might say that.

I arrived at the Texaco Building promptly at 10:00 A.M. and encountered an obstacle course in the main lobby. Due to a tense international situation, tight security measures were in place to prevent any sort of terrorist activity. Metal detectors, a set of camera shots matched to signatures, and careful scrutiny of personal identification all conveyed the impression that we were living in a tense age.

I then was escorted to the receptionist who asked me the nature of my business with Texaco.

I replied that I was in the field of education and had no particular business with Texaco.

It was at this point that a little layer of ice began to form on her words.

"Well then. What is the purpose of your visit to the Texaco?"

I replied that I hoped to have a little personal visit with Mr. Card.

"Was Mr. Card expecting you at this time?"

"Not really," I answered.

I was beginning to get an uncomfortable feeling about my visit. The next exchange only added to my conviction that I should have made an appointment.

"Mr. Card is extremely busy," she explained. "I am afraid that it might not be possible for you to just 'drop in' to see him without some type of advance preparation."

I knew that she was only doing her job, and I felt embarrassed that I was placing her in such an awkward situation (which she seemed to enjoy, I must add).

I suggested that she might call Mr. Card's secretary and see if by chance he had left word about me. To my surprise she took me up on the suggestion and almost immediately handed me the phone. Mr. Card's personal secretary introduced herself, apologized for any inconvenience I had experienced, and immediately "put me through" to the head man.

After explaining that his office was full of Arab oil tycoons who had undergone extensive security checks when they came there, he suggested that we might find it easier to meet downstairs than for me to have to go through all of those additional checks. He would be right down.

Now came the golden moment. I only hope the Lord has forgiven me the tacky sense of triumph I felt when I handed the receiver to the receptionist.

In her best "I tried to tell you and you wouldn't listen" posture, she asked, "Well, does he want you to come right up?"

"No," I replied. "Mr. Card said he would just come down here instead. He doesn't want me to go to a lot of trouble because of him."

The spirit of things then underwent an immediate change.

"Could you point him out to me when he gets close to us?" she asked almost apologetically. "I do not even know what he looks like."

It was only later when the visit was over that I noted some striking similarities between my day at Texaco and my walk with the Lord.

- It is not always easy to get from where we are to the throne of the Father.
- The Father is never too busy to share time with us.
- Anon Card was willing to leave the executive suite to come to me.
- Many of us who claim to know Jesus, including many who "work for Him," are not able to recognize Him.

Whatever Happened To Wise Old People?

Whatever happened to the tradition of seeking out a wise old person in the neighborhood in times of distress to determine the proper course of action to follow?

Where did the venerable old members go that used to make up a community's "spit and whittle club"?

When did we lose the host of veterans of troubled times who could be counted upon to give us a road map through difficult contemporary problems?

Every neighborhood used to have a stoved-up old cowboy who could always be counted on for a good story that illustrated a profound truth for youngsters to remember. On West Fourth Street in Borger we had old Smoky, a veteran of blizzards, rattlesnake bites, bucking horses, and bad women.

The kids would gather in the summer evening between the Cassidy house and the Bybees and form a line. For an hour or so, Smoky would sit in a cane bottom chair and unfailingly rope each and every left leg as the kids ran past him.

Smoky somehow seemed the final word on any subject or question that might arise.

I don't see many of his kind around any more, except on occasional visits to Washington and during TV newscasts.

Every college used to have a wise old saint who could always be counted on to recall the most minute detail of campus events from the vantage point of five decades of watching the student parade go by.

That wise old saint at Mississippi College was named Lightnin'. Old Doctor Nelson was finishing almost fifty years of service to the school, a good portion of that as president. Lightnin' was the only person on the campus who could remember when Dr. Nelson had come there.

Lightnin' used to "hold court" on the steps of Nelson Hall at 11:00 A.M. every Friday. Held in awe and sincerely respected by every student, Lightnin' never failed to meet the test of the most inquiring young mind.

His homespun wisdom was typified by his response to an inquiry about the speed with which he undertook his chores on the campus. With an obvious reference to his name, he was asked if he ever did anything "fast."

"Yes," he responded, "I get tired fast."

Whatever happened to the supply of wise old retired ministers who could, and would, take the time to listen to the fiery young evangelists who tried to "set the woods on fire" and learned that the wood was too green to burn?

One of my treasured memories is that of a visit to the home of a retired Presbyterian minister in Spearman, Texas, in 1953. Reputedly over ninety years of age, he had a well-earned reputation of being a good listener first, and a good advisor second, which may explain why there is such a shortage of these folks now.

As part of an organization called the Volunteer Mission Band from Wayland Baptist College, our group felt any visit north of Stinnett was incomplete without a stopover at his humble home.

When asked about his favorite pastorate, he always mentioned a well-known Presbyterian church in Highland Park. When asked why he treasured his rich memory of his experiences there, he replied that everyone in that church practiced tithing.

As expected, his astonishing revelation invariably brought a second question. How did he explain such a wonder?

His response was always the same, and was accompanied by a twinkle in each eye.

A few gave the tithe willingly. The Lord had to drag it out of the rest of them. But everyone tithed.

An Appropriate Monument

On November 9, 1923, there unfolded in the heart of Munich a near comic opera of events centering upon the aspirations of Adolf Hitler. A few hundred feet from the Marienplatz, with its Glockenspiel and other symbols of old Bavaria, a band of Hitler's followers made their way through the Residenzstrasse to the open plaza in front of the Temple of Odeon.

Shots were exchanged between about one hundred police and Hitler's followers, leaving sixteen Nazis and three police officers dead or dying.

Most historians of the Rise and Fall of Nazi Germany point to this event as the beginning of an unquenchable flame of hate and destruction that ultimately claimed the lives of forty million human beings.

I recently stood at the corner where Residenzstrasse opens into the Odeonplatz. I recalled a 1923 newspaper picturing the body of a Nazi lying at that very spot. This was the place where the first Nazi surrendered his life for the Fuehrer.

I could not help but note that the spot where the first shedding of blood occurred was marked *by a trash can*.

Back up the Residenzstrasse, after a turn or two, one comes to the Marienplatz and the beautiful fountain next to the steps leading to the subway system.

At this fountain, twenty-eight adult converts to the preaching of the Gospel were given a choice nearly five hundred years ago. They could recant their conversion and baptism, and be spared, or they could hold to their beliefs and be drowned in the fountain.

To a person, they held to their faith and paid the ultimate sacrifice for confessional obedience.

By dying in this manner, the believers joined the ranks of multiplied thousands who have had to determine not only what was worth their dying but also what was worth their living.

I could not keep from comparing the two unmarked historical spots. I also was caused to wonder what might be used to "mark" my grave that would place my life in a worthy context?

> By dying in this manner, the believers joined the ranks of multiplied thousands who have had to determine not only what was worth their dying but also what was worth their living.

Surprise!

A story made the rounds a while back about a woman who paid a visit to a horse ranch and bought a very expensive horse. The rancher was somewhat mystified when the address for delivery turned out to be in the center of a very elegant Dallas neighborhood. The new owner met the rancher at the door and told him to bring the animal into the house, up the stairway, and into the shower stall of the bathroom.

The final set of instructions compounded the mystery. The rancher was instructed to shoot the horse.

When asked why, the new owner gave a very plausible answer.

Her husband was due home in a few minutes. He would follow his usual rigid schedule and proceed to the bath upstairs to wash for dinner. Then he would come running down the stairs shouting, "There's a dead horse in the bathroom!"

And for the first time in their married life she would be able to say, "Yes, dear. I know."

Every husband longs for the day when he can spring a surprise on his wife and do so in such a way that it will create a feeling which will last for all of the remaining days of their marriage.

The longer two folks are married, the less chance the husband has of a genuine surprise. Maybe they see it in the corner of the eye. Perhaps it comes from batting zero for eighty-five.

In 1996 after nearly forty years of married life, I actually thought I had found a way to surprise Margie. I mean, I believed that I would *really* surprise Margie.

One of my responsibilities as director of the Christian Education Coordinating Board of the Baptist General Convention was to act as liaison between the Texas Baptist Historical Committee and the Texas Baptist Historical Society. This committee had oversight of a variety of organizations committed to the preservation of the history of Texas Baptists.

I was asked to serve as editor for the publication of a new edition of Z. N. Morrell's *Flowers and Fruits in the Wilderness* which led to a working relationship with Ed Eakin, the heart and soul of Eakin Press in Austin, Texas.

In the course of several working sessions in which Ed and I exchanged a lot of tall Texas tales, Ed asked me if I by chance had any of my stories in manuscript form. My affirmative response resulted in a contract offer from Ed to publish approximately one hundred of my historical anecdotes and sermon illustrations under the title, *Elmer and the Peas.*

I could hardly contain my sense of excitement as I made my way from Austin to Arlington.

Aside from my book, *Friedrich Schleiermacher: The Evolution of a Nationalist,* all of my publishing had been as editor, as in the case of *Flowers and Fruits.*

I could hardly wait to see her eyes light up as I handed Margie the contract. Wouldn't she be surprised!

Well, not really. She was pleased, but hardly surprised. As she said, it was just a matter of time until Ed and I got together on what struck her as a natural outgrowth of my background and interests.

As *Elmer and the Peas* progressed toward publication, I

became aware of the fact that Margie was intimately aware of most of the material in the book. Many of the experiences in the book involved her. Years of after-dinner addresses and sermons added to her reservoir of my materials. Finally, proof reading in search of her opinion about the material made it almost impossible for me to surprise her in any way with the final work.

There was one—and only one—way I could *finally* and completely surprise her. I would dedicate the book to her.

That would do it!

Victory would be mine. She would open the first book off the press, turn to the first page, and see a loving tribute to Margie, my beloved wife.

That would be a surprise.

My secret remained intact as the presses rolled, and the advance copies of my new creations were delivered.

With inexpressible joy I watched Margie's face as she opened the book to the dedication page directly behind the foreword. She read the dedication, turned a unique shade of red, and looked me straight in the eye.

"Who is Marie?" she asked as she handed me the book.

There it was for the Lord and everybody to see.

Dedication

To a VERY patient and long-suffering wife
Marie
who has endured multiple exposures
to the contents of this book and
responded with genuine appreciation on each
and every rendition

To accommodate space requirements Ed Eakin had moved my dedication box to a new location and had retyped the script. He somehow managed to omit the letter "g" from Margie. The result was a book dedicated to Marie.

I had hoped for a complete surprise.

It seems accurate to say that I had achieved my objective.

Would it be worth a line or two to point out that many of

our life-long dreams produce the same results? Dreams and a sense of humor go together.

Pickles

I joined the teaching faculty of Texas A&M University in August of 1968.

The first and most lasting impression I received was that the school was the classic example of an institutional split personality.

Every person I met on campus was either the world's leading authority on something (Bluford Hancock knew more about pecans than any person on earth) or seemed destined to achieve that reputation in the near future (Phil Gramm officed one floor up from me in Nagle Hall).

In the midst of excellence there was an almost pervasive fear of being some variation of an Aggie joke. General Earl Rudder, president of Texas A&M, led the university in the same courageous way he led the Rangers up the cliffs of Normandy on D-Day. When shown an error in spelling on the cover of a commencement program the evening before graduation ceremonies, he did not hesitate in ordering the mobilization of resources to completely reprint and distribute a new version, even though it kept several hundred people busy the entire night.

The result of the interaction of these conflicting emotions often led to hilarious situations, especially when it came to interviewing prospective additions to the faculty or administrative staff.

During a search for a new dean in Liberal Arts, the committee decided to take on the "Aggie" image and deal with it immediately. Each candidate was taken to lunch at ARNOLD'S, a barbecue place directly across from the main entrance to the campus.

ARNOLD'S was a tradition in College Station. Everything

about the place, such as the custom of attaching butcher knives to the table by a long chain, seemed to personify the crude side of Aggieland. While the candidate was evaluating a future at A&M, the committee was evaluating his or her reaction to this environment.

Thus the stage was set for the funniest event I have ever witnessed during a candidate interview.

Six members of the search committee were seated down one side and at the end of the table. The dean of Education and Liberal Arts was seated at the head of the table, and the prospective dean was seated alone to his left.

By arrangement with the waiter, each person was served a large dill pickle on a stick. After the waiter removed the stick, the pickle was left in the middle of a plate before each of the diners.

No food.

No bread.

No salad.

Just a great big dill pickle.

What would our noted scholar and prospective dean do with the pickle?

After a lengthy period of obvious discomfort, our guest concluded that all of this was for his benefit. He picked up his chained-to-the-table butcher knife in his right hand and plunged his fork into the pickle.

What he could not possibly have known was that the pickle, without the stick, was actually a salty gun barrel pointed toward the dean of Education and Liberal Arts. As soon as he pressed the fork into the pickle, juice squirted out that pickle's barrel and found a home dead center on the necktie of the dean.

Interview over!

Search over!

When I had time to think about it without laughing, I had a haunting suspicion that I had done the same sort of thing a number a times when I was trying to deliver a sermon.

Grace and the Law

The call came from the office of the head of Baylor Medical which was located only a five-minute walk from my office in the Baptist Building in Dallas. The day for which we all had been praying was about to become a reality, and our "family" was going home. The caller felt sure I would want to be there to tell them goodbye.

"Them" referred to a young couple, both still in their teens, and their baby son.

I had come to know them because of a brief interim pastorate a hundred miles from Dallas. Both came from ranching backgrounds, and each had the traditional Texas cowboy look about them.

They had married about the time I completed my work there, and a little more than a year later they had a precious little boy.

Within a few months of birth the precious child became the object of heroic efforts by the superb Baylor medical community. Five major surgeries followed, and I was pleased to be part of what was—I hope—a final goodbye to the hospital and hello to home for the family.

I shall never forget the scene that transpired in the hospital room.

Boone Powell, CEO of Baylor Medical, had the young couple sit for a moment for a word of prayer. Then he told them that he had two duties to perform before they went home.

First, he had to give them a final bill. The bill indicated that the series of major surgical procedures and the hospital stay left the family owing Baylor approximately $400,000.

As Dr. Powell said, he was meeting the letter of the law by giving them the bill.

I could not help but cry. If this young mother and dad both worked to the limit of their abilities for the rest of their lives, they would still never be able to pay the bill they owed.

Then Dr. Powell said that where the law ended, grace began. He handed them another bill showing the immense bill they owed, but with the words PAID IN FULL written across it.

God's people had paid the debt for them. Churches and their members all across Texas had made it possible for them to take their baby home and raise him in the nurture and admonition of the Lord.

The look on the faces of young mom and dad said it all.

After the last hug or two, and a bunch of tears, and a quiet time alone in the room before walking back to the office, I could not help but wonder.

> Who in their right minds would have refused to have their debts paid? Who on earth would have elected to work off their debt, fairly owed, knowing that the obligation had already been met?

Who in their right minds would have refused to have their debts paid? Who on earth would have elected to work off their debt, fairly owed, knowing that the obligation had already been met?

Who would choose the law over grace?

Get On Board Little Children

Community service seldom goes over-rewarded.

But then, the nature of community service is such that reward is seldom part of the equation anyway.

Evan, a friend for more than twenty years, has always been one of those guys who ends up on the list when the kids need a playground, a pancake supper needs cooks, the band needs new uniforms, or the synagogue needs new carpet.

It was not a surprise when he received a visit from sponsors who were trying to organize a Boy's Club and a Girl's Club in their city.

This time the request went beyond the day, the fund drive, or the performance. They were looking for someone to serve on their board of directors. They made it abundantly clear that it would be demanding and frustrating, but they promised an immense personal satisfaction as a result of his labors.

Evan thought it over, discussed it with his family, and concluded that this would not be asking too much of him. The kids were worth it. The community had been good to him, and this gave him the chance to repay an honest obligation.

He was told to meet with the nominating committee at the community center for a luncheon and business session prior to official election to their board.

Arriving at the appointed time and place, he asked the receptionist the location of the nominating committee. She answered by pointing to an open door at the end of the foyer where people had already assembled.

When he entered the room, the speaker motioned him toward the only vacant chair, and the meal began.

The speaker assured the gathering that the credentials of each person had been the object of intense scrutiny and that the responsibilities of the board were well within their range of capabilities. It was his privilege to announce that each person present was hereby elected to serve on the board of trustees.

It was then and only then was it mentioned that the board to which they were being elected was the governing board of the local university.

He had only missed the meeting of the nominating committee for the Boy's Club by one door.

Seems like I remember a day on the Sea of Galilee when Jesus was putting his "board" together.

Somewhere along the line they quit fishing and got down to serious business.

Shouldn't we all?

The Brotherhood of All Mankind

No visit to New York City is complete without a stop at the United Nations.

Come to think of it, no trip to New York City is complete under any circumstances, now that MAMA LEONE'S is no longer there.

The United Nations is a result of the unfulfilled dream of civilization for an orderly world.

The fact that the dream has stayed alive in spite of the best efforts to bring it into reality is a testimony to the perseverance of the human spirit.

I got a clue to the basic problem facing the United Nations on my one and only experience there.

We were in the coffee shop on the lower level near the main entrance. The counter was built in a small half-circle, and from our vantage point we could watch representatives of most of the world's inhabitants pass in review.

As the Dawsons and the Ogilvies enjoyed their coffee they also were somewhat amused by an exchange of barbed comments between a customer next to us and the waitress.

What started as a private disagreement about the quality of the coffee and the talents of the waitress for making anything fit to drink quickly escalated into a more philosophical explanation about each other's questionable ancestry.

As a final act of disdain, our fellow customer turned to us and in her most insulted demeanor said, "Greeks! What should one expect!"

With what she assumed was the end of the confrontation, she turned from the counter and walked away with an air of ultimate victory.

She almost made it.

With exquisite timing, the waitress turned to her audience of four and said with precisely enough volume to reach the ears of the departing customer, "Turks! They don't even know coffee!"

It may never be possible to straighten out the mess in the

general assembly upstairs until you can get them to agree about something, or anything, downstairs.

And when we get a formula for the UN, we might devote a little on our church "downstairs."

It surely adds value to the fact that in Christ there is "one faith, one hope, one promise."

Making the Right Choice

Phi Alpha Theta is the national honor society for historians. Achievement in undergraduate studies, as well as graduate school, is rewarded by election to a local chapter of the society and this, in turn, entitles one to membership in the national organization.

National annual meetings of Phi Alpha Theta provide outlets for the results of research and presentation of programs or plans to enhance the study of history.

The national meetings are augmented by regional Phi Alpha Theta conferences in various regions of the nation. These meetings are forums for showcasing bright undergraduates before those with the power to offer graduate scholarships, teaching fellowships, and special appointments to research centers and libraries.

Wayland Baptist College had been the recipient of a special grant from a very discerning donor who stipulated that the funds should be used to recruit a special class of bright young scholars without regard to financial need. Not surprisingly a class of unusually bright and highly motivated young people came to Plainview in 1961 and 1962.

The History Department somehow managed to attract a good share of the majors from this exceptional group. By their junior and senior years our "pride and joy" were demonstrating research and writing skills of the kind usually associated with graduate studies.

It was the unanimous decision of the Division of Social Sciences that we should submit the papers of three of our history students to the program committee for the Regional Phi Alpha Theta Conference in Albuquerque, New Mexico. Participation was usually restricted to first-year graduate students from major southwestern universities, but this was practice rather than policy.

Much to our delight, but of no surprise, all three papers were accepted for the conference.

As the program materialized it became apparent that the Wayland students were the only undergraduates on the entire program. We knew this, but it was not obvious to anyone else.

I shall never forget the moment when we stood at the door of the meeting hall on the evening before the formal start of the conference. Three proud professors and spouses, three undergraduates who were due to demonstrate their skills before the graduate world, and about two hundred members of Phi Alpha Theta were in attendance.

As we stood in the entrance, it was like the parting of the Red Sea. To our immediate left at the end of the banquet hall was a bar. A free bar at that. It was already populated by ranks six deep, and the noise level indicated that service had already been pretty brisk for half an hour.

To our immediate right was a collection of silver coffee urns, ample supplies of cups, assortments of pastries, and not a single taker.

It seemed for a moment like one of those theatrical flashbacks where everything stands dead still.

The three students were slightly in front of us, and clearly visible from the bar. Everyone in the room seemed to stop and look their way. I have never discussed with the others about how they felt, but I felt like a ham sandwich at a Hebrew picnic.

It was like their careers as graduate students, and all of the little elements that go into the career mix that results in doctoral work, were at stake.

Certainly, the greatest professorial pride I have ever felt came over me as our three young scholars turned without hesitation and walked in unison to the coffee urn (and two of them did not even like coffee).

They had no more than filled their cups and turned to

look toward the bar, when a fellow at the noisy end of the hall put down his drink and made his way down to us. It is still not clear whether his remark when he got there was a compliment or an accusation.

"Mercy, you Baptists are a pain. Here, give me a cup. I don't like to drink anyway."

His one-man trickle became a fifty-person flood. By the time the doors opened for the banquet, there were ten or twelve folks still at the free bar, and the rest were with us at the other end of the hall.

Like so many decisions of great significance in life, our young scholars did not wait until a critical moment to decide the important things in their lives.

If you have to ponder a long time before you can make ethical and moral decisions, the moment passes you by.

Everybody Needs a Hyphen

If asked about the work of a painter name Young-Hunter, most people would admit to a total ignorance about the man.

If shown a reproduction of one of Young-Hunter's paintings, most people would immediately recognize the painting, but they would not be able to remember where they had seen it.

If given the clue that they should picture in their mind the post office in their home town, most people would immediately place the painting on the wall above the door leading into the postmaster's office.

John Young-Hunter is a legend. From an aristocratic British background to a sick traveler seeking the "cure" in Taos, New Mexico, Young-Hunter made an amazing transition to become part of the American scene.

The West fascinated him. Wagons and wagon trains, settlers moving west, Indian children, scouts in camp—all came to life under his skilled brushes.

The New Deal era and commissions for "Post Office Art" did for his career what portrait painting alone could never have done. It made him an artist who touched the life of almost everyone in America in some way or another.

Taos was his laboratory as well as his home. And his home in Taos was a warehouse and a workshop for young talents who constantly passed that way.

After his death, his wife maintained the residence and what had become a teaching laboratory for artists as well as combination art museum and gallery. Finally, she elected to find an institution that would enter into a trust agreement to keep the Young-Hunter collection intact and operate the Taos location as a teaching center for artists, utilizing funds available in the trust to support the entire venture.

Showings were arranged at a number of Southwestern universities and colleges, including a stop at Wayland Baptist College in Plainview.

Prior to the appointment at Wayland, the collection was to be shown at a major regional university, which put its "best foot forward" to make a favorable impression regarding that school's ability to provide a worthy residence for the Young-Hunter Trust.

Someone slipped just a tad. A dean was officially sent to open the collection and the showing of family memorabilia. The dean made one little mistake in his opening remarks. He referred to Young-Hunter as an American Indian instead of portraying him as a member of the British nobility who painted American Indians.

Could that have been the reason Mrs. Young-Hunter left the festivities?

The next day the entire collection had been crated and shipped.

Wayland eventually became the host institution for the Young-Hunter Collection. A dean at another school is still wondering why folks do not like Indian artists.

The prophet said of Jesus that he came unto his own, and his own received him not. And he never had a hyphen in his name.

Who Needs a Thumb?

A trademark for a career in the oil fields is a stub where the thumb ought to be.

By definition, a career in the oil fields used to be eight years. That was how long it took, on the average, to lose a thumb. It was about ten years for the index finger.

It was easy to find old roughnecks in the domino halls. Old veterans had to stand their dominoes on their side, because they could not palm seven "rocks" without both thumbs. And if they had both thumbs, they would not be hanging around the domino hall in the first place.

Three likely accidents would have been the cause of lost fingers and thumbs. The chain used to "make up" drill stem (by screwing it into place at the joint) was enemy number one. It usually was the most dangerous when a "boll weevil" (someone new to a drilling rig floor) was learning. The second time of danger was the first tour on Monday morning after the crew had devoted a good portion of the weekend to the bottle.

If throwing the chain did not claim a thumb, winch lines did. Everything in the oil fields is either heavy, slick, or jagged. A winch line was the standard means of lifting and moving these objects, and many a hand got in the way of things as the line was tightened, loosened, or otherwise adjusted.

The third villain was the device used to connect a trailer to a truck. Every device used in oil field work is pulled, hauled, or driven to the point where the work is done. Literally dozens of techniques were used over the years, and all failed the safety test. Nubs and trucks just seemed to go together.

That is, they all failed the coupling test until Tommy Greenway came along. Tommy was one of those likable fellows who could do just about anything in the oil patch. He owned and operated his own welding shop for years on Tenth Street in Borger, Texas, and joined the fraternity of thumbless good-old-boys one day while making up a truck and trailer.

What was the stopping place for everyone else became the

starting place for Tommy. Flo, his always affectionate and sometimes cussing wife, maintained faith in him when a lot of people were willing to consign him to a desk at the shop.

Tommy set out to prove that he could hook a trailer to a truck while working alone.

All existing connections required two people—one to drive the truck, and one to pull the pin that fell in place when the truck was backed into place against the trailer.

Not only was Tommy determined to prove that you did not need a thumb to pull the pin, he was determined to prove that you could connect the truck to the trailer without any help at all.

It took months, and head scratching galore, and many a soapstone sketch on the concrete floor, but Tommy Greenway finally did it.

He invented the fifth wheel.

The fifth wheel became the standard device for connecting a truck to a trailer. The amazing thing about it was its simplicity of operation. The rights to the patent brought Tommy and Flo a standard of living on a plain with the union leaders and the big ranchers and royalty owners of Borger, but Tommy never forgot that a badly mashed thumb was his gateway to opportunity.

I would never be so bold as to point out the obvious, but there was a lot of spunk required in addition to an immense faith in the hearts of the disciples when the Cross crushed their hopes at Calvary.

One doesn't have to visit many of the church "domino halls" to realize that there are great hosts of nubby former workers still nursing injured parts of their ministry.

And many a church is waiting today for someone to find a way around a hurt so that member can become a productive member of the fellowship.

Good Advice?

Mother was the smallest of the whole Gibson clan, measuring two inches neigh of five feet. She had to stand on tiptoes to be short. If she had been any shorter she would not even have touched the floor.

She may have been short of inches, but she was never short of opinions.

Strangely enough, I do not recall a great many words of advice that come by way of my mother. I say it is strange, because my mother's family was solid Irish and utterly without reservations in their self-confidence.

I rather believe that most of her words of wisdom were passed on in my early years and with genuine gentleness.

The one really wise bit of advice I remember her giving was in 1952 when I had taken Margie as my bride, and we were off to Wayland Baptist College to begin what has been a life-long involvement in education.

With only a sixth grade education to her credit, Mother was acutely aware of the fact that I was heading down a path mostly unknown to her.

So what does a wise and proud Mother say to a newly-married, green-as-a-gourd son that will help him when Mother is not there to be of assistance?

"Always remember, son," she said. **"Eat to the left and drink to the right. It will keep you from embarrassing yourself."**

How many times have I sat at a round banquet table and noticed that seven sets of eyes were slyly watching to see which napkin I picked up? Thanks, Mom.

On one such occasion, a special dinner for Gov. Bill Clements at East Texas Baptist University, I was acutely aware of the fact that virtually everyone at the head table was waiting for me to "make the first move."

A simple truth dawned upon me. If people were watching me to keep from making some trivial social false move, what else were they observing? Or imitating?

There is a tremendous difference between using the correct fork and taking the correct fork in the road.

The Scriptures picture the rich young ruler who came to Jesus seeking to know what "else" he needed to do to inherit eternal life. When Jesus told him to narrow the focus of his life to following Him, the seeker went away in a sad state.

Critical choices in our life are not always that dramatic. Sometimes it takes years before we see validation and affirmation in the results of the choices we have made. More often than not, the consequences of our choices are immediate.

Eat At Joe's

Several years ago we were making our way across southwestern Colorado at the conclusion of a great vacation of trout fishing and mountain climbing.

Making our way east toward Monarch Pass, we began to notice signs advising one and all to eat at JOE'S. (Trout)

The farther we went the bigger the signs were. **Don't Miss JOE'S.** (Trout).

Then the signs became specific. **Eat Trout at JOE'S!** (Trout)

Remember that you are seeing these signs through the eyes of a guy who ties his own flies! (Trout)

We made our way through a magnificent pass, past aspen groves, through stands of spruce, down a boulder and pine canyon, and across the same stream which was rapidly becoming a river. (Trout)

Now the signs were more specific.

FIVE MILES to the World's Finest Trout!
TWO MILES to a Trout FEAST!
YOU ARE GOING TO MISS IT IF YOU DON'T SLOW DOWN!

And then, have mercy, there it was. Log buildings, smoke gently rising from two chimneys, deep green grass, aspen and spruce highlighting the filtered sunlight, and a rolling trout haven beside it all. **JOE'S.**

Without a doubt this was the most picturesque trout place I had ever seen. And the inside was better than the outside view. Checkered tablecloths, mounted wild game on the walls, huge fireplaces, and views of the roaring trout river—everything said the signs about eating at **JOE'S** were "right on the money."

One glance around the room revealed a considerable collection of "good ol' boys" absolutely lost in the pursuit of heaped up plates of fried trout with all the traditional sacrifices to the god of gluttony.

When the waitress tried to give us menus we had already made up our minds. Trout and lots of it for the entire Dawson gang.

There is really no need to recount the search and destroy operation our table witnessed when we were served. It was everything we had wanted and then some.

The fact that I remember this one particular trout feast after three decades is a testimony to two things.

First, great meals with your family in an ideal setting are "memory makers." We all need to work on that part of our life. Margie, Kim, Carey, and Jamie all agreed with me that this was about the most perfect trout dinner we had ever experienced.

Second, images of perfection are seldom what they seem.

When the waitress brought us our ticket, I pointed to the stream outside and asked if by chance these trout had been taken from their own personal trout supply.

"Oh, no," she replied with great exuberance. "We fly them in from Houston."

Life is filled with special moments that offer deep personal spiritual experiences which can best be enjoyed without too much inquiry into "where the trout came from."

Just Wearing the Uniform

A mission trip to Germany was behind us and a few days of relaxation were ahead of us when we used our Urail passes to make our way from Cologne, Germany, to Limerick, Ireland, by way of Brussels, Paris, and Cherbourg.

We purposely elected to take the ferry across the Irish Sea from Cherbourg to Ireland because of the recommendations from many different sources that this was a very relaxed and trouble-free way to get there.

In the usual timely manner, our train from Paris arrived at the station in the port city of Cherbourg, and we boarded a bus for the short journey to the dock and our ferry.

The first hint I had that something was amiss was when two officers came to the bus and carried on a lengthy and somewhat animated conversation with the driver. Several French-speaking passengers near the front also seemed a little unsettled as word passed back through the bus that there might be a "problem" at the dock.

Apprehension turned to genuine concern when the bus entered the dock area and proceeded toward the Irish ferry waiting for us at the last berth.

There, squarely between the bus and the ferry, was a line of perhaps fifty motorcycles and their leather garbed owners forming a barrier across the only visible path to the boarding point for the ferry.

"Hell's Angels," said several folks in unison. True or not, nearly one hundred folks who would clearly pass for the cast of a Marlon Brando movie were beside their bikes, arms crossed, starring toward our bus in what was obviously meant to be a confrontation with authority.

At this point the officer in charge of the bus told us that we should not be alarmed. There was no point to be made by any type of confrontation. The bus would simply take an alternate route which would take us around the end of the line of bikers for a timely arrival at the ferry.

I was struck by the fact that the bikers never seemed to see our bus. It was as though they were alone on the dock and oblivious to our presence.

Whatever crisis there might have been never developed, and whoever keeps score on this sort of event obviously chalked one up for arrogance and incivility.

Two days later we were seeing the traditional sights at Bunratty Castle and King John's Castle in Limerick. The folks at the tourist center at John's Castle could not have been more accommodating, even to the point of calling a cab for us. They assured us that the driver who was coming for us was a gentleman of the first order, and we should not hesitate to ask of him any favor to make our trip more enjoyable.

Their confidence in the driver seemed to be well placed. He was a tourist's delight with manners to match his vast knowledge about historical points of interest.

When he got around to asking how long we had been in Ireland, I responded that we had only spent two days there, having come on the ferry from Cherbourg.

"What a coincidence," he responded. He, too, had been on that very same ferry. He liked to come home that way because they took such good care **of his bike.**

Yes. He had been one of the Hell's Angels who confronted the bus at the wharf at Cherbourg.

As politely as possible I mentioned that there seemed to be a fantastic transformation from the biker on the wharf to the cabby driving us. What had happened to that shaggy, arrogant, trouble-making rascal we had seen at Cherbourg?

Oh, that! He had simply changed uniforms. He assumed that we all do that from time to time.

When we were joined at Bunratty by George and Nettie Ramsey, Bob and Mary Jean Hazlett, and Jim and Leona Smith, we shared the experience at the wharf with them. Soon we began to notice that almost everyone we saw wore some type of "uniform."

Ultimately we were forced to consider our own behavior to see if what we affirmed and professed was a good reflection of what we were.

Did not Jesus say something about people who have a white shiny uniform which conceals a tomb filled with dead men's bones?

Been There Too Long

I accepted an appointment as dean of the Graduate School at Southwest Texas State University in July of 1971.

Shortly thereafter I represented my institution at a regularly scheduled meeting of the Coordinating Board, an appointed body charged with oversight of higher education in the State of Texas.

The meeting occurred on the campus of McClendon County Community College in Waco. The first item on the agenda was a request from one of the tax-supported junior colleges for special consideration with regard to formula funding.

This particular college wanted to retain its traditional "quarter" system for offering courses in contrast with the semester system used at all other tax-supported institutions in Texas.

Interestingly enough, after only a very brief discussion of the request, it became apparent to everyone in the chamber that no one on the Coordinating Board had the foggiest notion of what constituted a "quarter hour" of study.

The request was quickly dealt with, if for no other reason than the need to avoid any further embarrassment on the part of the highest educational authority in higher education in Texas.

In short order a second thorny proposal came to the attention of the Coordinating Board.

Several counties had joined forces to try to establish a junior college in West Texas. The rules for basic numbers of scholastics needed to support such a request had delayed the efforts for years. Finally, careful calculations of the previous year's scholastics had indicated that state mandates had been met, barely, and a delegation representing the population of this vast region was present to petition the board for authority to proceed with the necessary elections and bonding steps to establish a school.

The delegation seemed to be cut from a Larry McMurtry book on life in West Texas. They had the look of good folks with a dream about to come true.

Testimony proceeded along predictable lines, with weaknesses and strengths on both sides of the request being recited.

Then an officer of the county court from one of the key counties in the proposed junior college district asked to be heard.

His testimony was brief and unassuming. He "allowed as how" his statement before the Coordinating Board would cost him his job in the next county election, but he asked the board to turn down the request "for the time being."

His reason?

Those kids had already lived there for eighteen years!

Consideration for the proposal resulted in a motion and a second for postponement and reconsideration at a future time.

I was struck by the basic forum which our democracy presented to those who had a dream and those who wanted others to pursue another dream. I was also impressed by the difficulties inherent in determining when someone, or churches, or denominations, or groups of someones, have been "there" too long.

Just a thought.

Things That Go Bump in the Night

In its early boom days from 1926 until the decade after World War Two, Borger, Texas, was a pretty tough town.

The town started "from scratch" in 1926, with no community structure of any kind upon which to build an orderly society. Borger went from bare prairie to 40,000 people in only a few months. People came to try their hand at making money and left as soon as they could.

My folks were living in Canyon during the boom and concluded that they surely could do better in the oil fields than the farm and dairy where they were barely existing. They arrived in Borger on the so-called Doodlebug (one car train) at the station next to the Black Hotel at noon on a Saturday.

The first two people Frank and Nellie Dawson saw when they got off the train were stark naked, and one was chasing the other with a butcher knife.

My nineteen-year-old father took his sixteen-year-old wife, and the two of them got right back on the train to return to Canyon. Things were hardly any more civilized when they returned two years later and stayed, this time to build a home and a life.

Much of the early rowdiness came under some semblance of order after martial law was imposed by army troops from Fort Worth.

I say "semblance" because there was a constant threat of violence lurking around every corner of Borger, and many of my earliest memories of Borger are associated with the life-style of my parents, and the environment they were part of.

My father was a welder by trade, and a floor bouncer by choice. Mother often worked selling drinks and set-ups while he "worked" the floor. Even as a youngster I was permitted to "hang around" the honky tonk until they got through, and we made our way home.

I recall all of this with the knowledge that my parents were good and gentle with Barbara, Nella Rose, and me. I have never been able to reconcile my father's enjoyment over the use of a blackjack and a total void of any type of corporal punishment with us.

In many respects he was a man of absolutes—right and wrong.

He was staunchly anti-union.

The only political statement I ever heard him make was said at the dinner table the day Germany surrendered in May of 1945. He sounded a lot like Patton when he allowed as how we ought to march right on in to Russia and take care of them while we were at it.

He strongly believed that people should mind their own business. When things went "bump" in the night in our neighborhood on West Fourth Street, he did not allow us to go see what it was about.

My earliest recollection of the sound of a dynamite blast relates to some union activity among a couple of families of

Indians in our neighborhood. I never really understood at the time that they were looked upon as scabs, but about midnight the windows shook at our house, and a powerful blast made the rounds. The next morning the house across the street and four houses west was minus a front porch.

Some folks said it must have been a gas leak. We were right on top of several pipelines, and the house where we lived was on lease land. Some even suggested that maybe some homemade liquor might have set itself off.

All I recall is that we were not permitted to discuss it at the table and were told that the "bump" was none of our business. Besides, we did not have a front porch.

And then one day God in his wisdom and mercy saw fit to enter into the heart of my father. The term "conversion" was never more appropriate to any person than it was to him. Like Paul and the people of Philippi, I thank God for every remembrance I have of my father once Frank A. Dawson met the Lord.

In what may seem a role reversal to some, it was my father who contributed to the spiritual growth of my mother. She was the first fruits of his walk with the Lord.

Save Some Time for Yourself

Howard Bennett was president of East Texas Baptist College for roughly eighteen years. Prior to his service at that noble school he was pastor of a succession of outstanding churches, culminating with his tenure at First Baptist Church in Kilgore.

Dr. Bennett's retirement concluded a presidency that was typified by the term used to describe him by all who knew him —gentleman.

When I assumed the responsibilities of president, I visited with Dr. Bennett out of a sincere respect for his statesmanlike qualities. I asked him if there might be any word of advice from him that would help me carry on the work he had started at the Marshall campus.

His response was typical of his personality and his life-style. He said that there was really not much he could tell me that would be of any use to me. He felt assured that I would want to do some things he had never thought of, and surely would want to talk to others about things not yet attempted.

Then he fell into what might best be described as a moment of reverie or introspection. After what seemed like five minutes as he "thought within himself," he added what I felt at the moment was an afterthought.

"Save some time for yourself. I did not do that. Now look at me."

It took a pretty good eye to detect what he was describing. The tremors, the shaky hands, the slumping of the frame —all pointed to the onset of a debilitating illness that progressed rapidly through the next few years.

Dr. Bennett remained true to his word. He never once broke his own pledge to let me find my own way through the presidential maze, although I am positive that there were times when he surely wanted to have "a word" with me for my own benefit.

Not long before his illness ran its course I went by their home to visit with Dr. and Mrs. Bennett to pay my respects.

Dr. Bennett seemed so small in the large easy chair. He was leaning to one side and slightly huddled, and his voice had grown so weak that I had to lean close to his chair to hear the gentleman speak.

He raised a finger and gestured for me to come even closer to him, and I responded by moving perhaps six inches from him.

The words he spoke were the last words I heard him say.

"Remember. Save some time for yourself."

His last words were words of concern for my welfare, and not his own.

I tried to tell Mrs. Bennett about the conversation after his funeral. Only then did I realize that he had demonstrated an almost Christ-like spirit on my behalf.

Give That Guy a Disease

An outbreak of equine encephalitis in Texas in 1962 and 1963 caught the attention of virtually everyone.

As the number of confirmed cases climbed past fifty in Plainview, and the total count numbered in the hundreds across the South Plains, virtually every available agency was recruited to help determine the source of the disease, the means of transmission, and any possible opportunities to minimize the terrible effect of the epidemic.

Migratory birds were considered to be the most probable source for the outbreak. Verification would require a massive effort to collect enough blood samples to reconstruct the path of transmission and infection.

Wayland Baptist College volunteered the services of its science faculty to assist in the gathering and testing of blood samples. Hale County and eight contiguous counties were to become a huge laboratory. In all, over nine hundred blood samples were to be drawn each month from birds in each of these counties, or one hundred per county per month.

Teams of volunteer hunters were recruited. Each team was furnished with a special permit to hunt without limit and without regard to hunting seasons. Most important of all, each team was given a letter of introduction concerning the emergency nature of the gathering of the blood samples. Obtaining samples could occur only after the team had secured written permission from the property owners or operators.

Only a high and noble cause like preventing an epidemic could explain the gathering that occurred on a farm near Summerfield on a very hot, extremely dry, and characteristically windy day in July.

I was joined by a motley renegade assembly made up of Junior Arterburn, Pete Claytor, Dan Law, Jerry Walker, Dr. Ed Kajihiro, and Dr. Charles Ogilvie.

Kajihiro, a native of Hawaii and of Japanese descent and a highly qualified scientist, accompanied Ogilvie, our team captain, to the front door of a very dilapidated frame farm house.

The long, lanky cowboy who answered the knock on the door proved to be an appropriate object of scientific study in his own right.

How had he managed to find the knob on the door? It was a sure bet that he had not been able to focus on anything in about three days.

How had he managed to get all of those beer bottles on the one kitchen table visible through the doorway?

What would his blood test prove about alcohol as a deterrent for infestations of mosquitoes? His was obviously a case of maximum exposure to beer, and he seemingly was free of mosquito bites.

Ed Kajihiro very patiently explained to our teetering host the nature of our mission and read to him the document granting to our party the necessary permission to gather blood samples.

Would he please repeat all of that?

Again, Kajihiro explained the purpose of the visit. Again, the fellow asked for further clarification.

After about five tries, he finally relented and agreed to sign the document granting permission to hunt on his property.

Now the mission focused on finding a flat surface where he could sign the paper.

Not very adept in moving around beer bottles, the crew pitched in to clear the table and seat our host, and soon we left with permission in hand.

Compared to the ordeal of seeking permission for the hunt, the remainder of the day was pretty routine, and resulted in specimens from ducks, mud hens, quail, pheasant, and a prairie chicken.

The shocker came the next day in the form of a call to Dr. Ogilvie from the sheriff's office.

The sheriff explained that they were investigating a strange report from the Summerfield area.

A local farmer had reported that a group of armed men had come to his farm with sinister motives. As he remembered it, they were trying to give encephalitis to a little Japanese fellow.

After a good laugh over the whole incident, Pete and

Junior pointed out painful but obvious parallels between our visit to the farm and the mission of Jesus to live among men.

There is an obvious state of emergency.

The blood of Jesus offered the only pathway to a remedy.

We have all the information we need to make the search for hope and help.

We all have to clear something from our table before we can "sign on."

Lay Up Treasures

On the surface most Baptist churches seem strikingly similar.

They conduct their services with an almost incredible fear of doing things "out of order" without acknowledging that habit and repetition are not necessarily ordained of the Lord.

When they dare to venture away from the time-honored, if not scriptural, order of service, they have a tendency to copy someone else who has ventured from the "true way" so as to be safe if the Lord starts striking errant churches with lightning. There is always safety in numbers.

When a church does venture into new territory, it is both noticeable and fraught with peril.

In the 1960s I served First Baptist Church of Abernathy, Texas, as interim pastor. Bro. Boyce Evans had served the church well, and good leadership from the church body made the interim a pleasant experience in every way.

The very predictable pastoral search process led the church in a very predictable way to invite Bro. Hubert Long to assume the duties of pastor. As soon as he had prayed about the call of the church, Bro. Long accepted and agreed to begin his ministry in four weeks.

All very ordinary to this point. Then came a surprise.

Leland Phillips, local banker and staunch deacon, asked me the most unusual question put to me in over sixty interim pastorates.

"Bro. Jerry, how or what can we do to really show a pastor that we appreciate him and his willingness to serve our church?"

I thought about it a while and finally said that they might want to consider among other things the fact that moving from Decatur, Texas, to Abernathy would probably deplete the grocery stocks pretty drastically. Perhaps the church should consider giving the pastor's family an old-fashioned food pounding. Everyone in the church could participate at whatever level they could afford, and it would be genuinely appreciated by the pastor's family.

Bro. Phillips beamed. Great idea!

And since I had suggested the pounding, it seemed appropriate to him and the rest of the deacons that I should personally head up the campaign. My job for four weeks would be to promote the food pounding to end all food poundings. Pull out all of the stops. Dance in the pulpit. Put folks on guilt trips. Threaten the wrath of God for even a sign of non-cooperation.

At last, here was a chance to be "different."

I must confess that it turned into one of the really "fun" experiences of my life.

The first announcements on Sunday number one were "predictable" to say the least. Sunday night seemed to need a "little something" so we pushed peanut butter and sardines.

Wednesday night prayer time seemed appropriate for some special recipes and weird things like artichoke hearts.

Sunday number two witnessed a personality change on the part of the congregation. Predictable had now become unpredictable, and I sensed a faint smile on otherwise staid faces.

By the time we got to the last Sunday of my tenure, we had taken our pitch to the level of the absurd. The more I pushed, the harder the congregation laughed. They could hardly keep from nudging each other in the ribs as I made the last fervent plea at the end of the final night service.

With my mission accomplished as interim pastor and a virtual avalanche of goodies awaiting the new pastor the next Sunday, I made my way to the rear of the auditorium and dutifully told the faithful goodbye.

Leland Phillips waited patiently for the last well-wisher to shake my hand, and then seemed to slip into a somber personality change. It seemed that there was a little matter of some money that had been contributed for food but unaccounted for. He hated to see my interim service end with a question mark hanging over things. At his request, but totally dumbfounded, I went with him back through the darkened hall to the dining room where we could "talk things out over a cup of coffee."

With that, we stepped into the pitch-dark and absolutely quiet fellowship hall and turned on a light.

SURPRISE!!!

Before me were assembled the men, women, children, staff, and strays of First Baptist Church of Abernathy, and in the center of the hall was an enormous pile of cans, sacks, jars, packages, and parcels. I had spent four weeks promoting my own food pounding.

My first thought way down in the depths of my soul?

I should have suggested a new car!

It also occurred to me that this was much like the admonition for us to lay up for ourselves treasures in heaven.

We get to promote our own heavenly pounding.

Do we serve a great God, or what?

Let's Talk About It

One of the most common skills required of any person pursuing a "call" to the ministry falls under the broad category of communication. And of all the types or variations of communication skills, the spoken word seems to be the variable most closely related to the length of time a minister stays in the ministry.

Successful churches are also required to demonstrate and practice good communication skills, and more often than not, these skills utilize group dynamics separate and apart from the individual skills of the pastor.

Unfortunately, pastors who are skilled at communicating with "the masses" and churches that succeed in building a positive image often find that they cannot communicate with each other.

We paid a visit to Margie's folks in the "four corners" region of northwest New Mexico and looked forward to attending services with my wife's family. I had not counted on a casual meeting with their pastor on Saturday afternoon.

It is a common ministerial courtesy for a pastor to invite a visiting minister to preach for him when they meet under our circumstances. It is also a generally accepted understanding that the invitation is merely a pleasantry and not to be taken seriously.

After we exchanged the traditional greetings and chatted about denominational trends and current health conditions of our respective families, the local pastor extended what I understood to be a courtesy invitation to preach for him the next day at the morning service.

I graciously declined and assured him that I needed to "feast on some home cooking" for a change.

At that point, after a glance around, he pressed the issue. He assured me that he was quite serious about the invitation.

"My deacons don't know it yet, but I am leaving pretty soon," he said. "It would do us all good to have a little change of pace, and I would deeply appreciate it," he continued with almost a sense of desperation.

Against my better judgment I agreed to speak the next morning, and we parted on that note.

The services the following day were a delight. Every effort was made by everyone in the church to make visitors feel welcome and "seekers" encouraged. Announcements were positive and concise, and I had the feeling that the church had a pretty healthy congregation.

Following the services and the traditional hand shaking, three men approached me and asked if I might spare them a moment of my time before I left.

I guess I should have anticipated what followed after we made our way to a room off the sanctuary.

"Our preacher doesn't know it yet, but he is leaving pretty soon," declared the spokesman. "Would you consider yourself a candidate when the vacancy occurs?"

It grieved my soul to realize that the pastor and his church were obviously skilled at communicating with the world but could not communicate with one another.

And if conversations between pastors and congregations seem convoluted, consider what often happens when we talk to our own soul.

Jesus talked about the man who talked to himself and congratulated himself for goods laid up for many years. His conclusion was that he would build bigger and better barns and enjoy things.

Using the strongest language possible to describe the foolhardiness of self-deception, Jesus cautioned that his soul would soon be required of him.

Dishonesty with one's self is the ultimate failure in communication.

Up and Walking Around

Mathematics is a very inexact science for many, many ministers. Do not ever ask a preacher how many people attended any given service if you have any expectation of receiving an accurate assessment.

By comparison, public relations is an art form that rises to profound heights when loosened from the bonds of exactitude.

One questionable secular account of the miracle of the parting of the waters of the Red Sea puts all of this in bold relief.

According to the unauthorized and certainly errant account, the Children of Israel were desperate when they got to the Red Sea and saw the army of the Pharaoh in close pursuit.

Moses quickly recognized the desperation inherent in the

situation and immediately ordered the Israelites to sit down while he petitioned the Lord on their behalf.

Returning from the edge of the Red Sea, Moses asked them, "What would you say if I were to tell you that in a little while I am going to stand beside the water and lift my staff in the air. The water will part, and all of you will be able to cross on dry ground. After you get across, I will follow. The army of the Egyptians will try to follow, but I will let my staff down, and the waters of the Red Sea will close over the army, and we will all be saved."

A hush supposedly fell over the Children of Israel. Then the director of public relations for the Children of Israel stood up and said, "Boss, if you can pull that off, I can get you three pages in the Old Testament."

There is a universal and almost irresistible urge among the ecclesiasticals to get three pages in the Old Testament.

One of the great names in pioneer Texas Baptist life belongs to Z. N. Morrell. More than any other minister he can be described as a founding father of the denomination.

The ultimate secular recognition was accorded Z. N. Morrell when his remains were moved to the State Cemetery in Austin for his role in the settlement of frontier

Texas. The burial site was marked by a temporary marker, but "temporary" turned into decades before the Texas State Historical Commission finally completed the task of honoring him with a permanent historical marker for the grave.

The formal ceremony marking the burial site was attended by a noteworthy assembly. It included over fifty denominational leaders, representatives from the press, descendants of Z. N. Morrell, and representatives of the Texas State Historical Society.

When the Administrative Staff of the Executive Board of the Baptist General of Texas met the following week, the first item of business was Dr. William Pinson's call for a report on the ceremony at the State Cemetery in Austin.

Tom Brannon, director of the Office of Communications, gave a very factual review of the activities of the day. When the question arose concerning attendance at the event, Tom very dutifully turned to me and asked, "Dr. Dawson, how many would you say were at the cemetery?"

Without hesitation I said that there were about five hundred and fifty at the cemetery.

Quite appropriately, and not wanting to get three pages in the Old Testament, Tom asked, "Are you sure about that? I only counted about fifty."

"Well, yes. Up and walking around," I responded without hesitation.

You Stole My Watch

The academic road leading to an earned doctorate is fraught with pits, pathos, and peril.

A majority of those who start a college degree program never graduate.

Half of those who complete their undergraduate programs seek admission to graduate studies, but only half of that number begin graduate level studies.

Of those who begin graduate level pursuit of a variety of degrees at the master's level, less than half complete their degree plan.

Half of those earning a degree at the master's level seek some type of admission to doctoral programs, and less than half of that number are admitted.

Four or more years of undergraduate studies are thus followed by two to four years of study at the master's level, and admission into doctoral programs requires three to five years of residence, service as a lowly teaching assistant or grader, and unending research on a topic upon which the completion of the doctorate is dependent.

And while every step of the educational pilgrimage exacts a toll of as much as fifty per cent, the final step leading to candidacy status has proved to be the most insurmountable barrier. Most members of the academic community, when asked their *worst* experience along the trail to their doctorate, will say *the last one*.

Of all the stops, traps, problems, barriers, and obstacles along the doctoral path, none is more subjective than the final judgment of a committee of educators who represent the closed society of the academic world. They hold the key to the door leading to admission to their academic club, and "everything" rides on their professional judgment, collective emotions, domestic tranquillity, and problematic ulcers. The fragile nature of the moment often times cannot bear the extra weight of something unexpected.

A classic example of the very worst case of the unexpected occurred while I was in the midst of my doctoral studies.

A retired army officer was up for his comprehensive exams in the field of American History. The graduate assistants in the department kept book on their peers seeking to advance to the dissertation level, and "Smith" was rated as better than even odds to make the transition on his first try for admission to candidacy.

Smith had some physical problems he had carried over from World War Two and Korea, namely, a slight hardness of hearing and a degree of harshness in his human relations. His memory was unfailing.

The University regularly structured doctoral candidacy committees to include someone who was neutral about, or completely unknown to, the candidate. In Smith's case the neutral member was a very distinguished visiting professor associated with the administration of the Fulbright scholarship program in Europe. As visiting professor in European History he was a logical selection.

During the normal course of introductions Professor "Friedrich" asked Smith if the two of them had not met somewhere before. There then followed the customary search for some common event that might have brought the two together, and then the committee got down to business.

Almost an hour into the oral examination, Professor Friedrich suddenly sat upright in his chair, pointed an accusing finger at Smith, and exclaimed, "I do, indeed, know you. You stole my watch!"

Professor Friedrich had been pressed into military service by the Germans and was part of a unit retreating toward the Po River at the very end of the war in 1945. He and his fellow platoon members stripped and loaded their belongings on to a raft and began swimming for the north bank, pushing the raft and their belongings ahead of them.

Smith's unit was right behind them and fired a round ahead of the raft, forcing the swimmers to give up their effort to flee. They returned to the bank, coming out of the water without benefit of clothing.

According to Herr Friedrich, "All I had on was my watch, and you stole it from me."

To say that this account by Herr Friedrich took the committee and the candidate by surprise is the understatement of the century.

And despite all of the assurances from Herr Friedrich that the past episode should have no bearing upon the continuation of the examination, it was over. It may not have been the end of the world, but it was most certainly the end of an academic career.

Speaking of ends of the world, the scriptures tell of another examination that Smith, and all of the Smiths of the world will experience.

It will be a final examination.

Every thought, every word, every deed will be recalled.

The greatest joy imaginable will come with the discovery that the test has already been taken by the Master on our behalf.

I Do Not Want to Live Like That

My father was one of those indestructible pioneer types. With only a sixth grade education he could do, build, or fix just about everything.

What he may have lacked in formal education he more than made up for with dogged determination.

I saw him lose his temper one time in my entire life.

I heard him laugh aloud the first time when I was thirteen years old.

I saw him change his mind once. Well, at least he altered his position once. He never changed his mind.

I still remember the day we walked from our tar-paper house on West Fourth Street to a plot of land only a block away on McGee Street. He told me that on that lot we were going to dig a hole fifty feet long, twenty-five feet wide, and eight feet deep.

Silly me. As a thirteen-year-old I had the temerity to ask who he meant when he said "we."

It took almost a year, but we did it. Hired help was a waste of resources. "We" did it.

He dearly loved the house he had put together from two "shotgun" shacks, the lumber salvaged from two honky tonks in White Deer, and lumber liberated from a dozen bull wheels.

If he loved anything as much as he loved that house, it was Calvary Baptist Church.

I was perturbed but not surprised in the summer of 1991 when Papa called me and told me he had been having dizzy spells that day. Dizzy spells at age eighty-two are not unusual.

In fact, dizzy spells are a regular part of life for a man eighty-two years old who has spent a hot summer day on the roof of the shed which houses Calvary's church van.

When I said he just might drop dead the next time he tried that stunt, that old Choctaw singleness of mind gently slid into place.

"That's okay with me," he said. And he meant it.

When I came home to Arlington in November from the Baptist State Convention in Waco, there was a call waiting. I instinctively knew that my dad was about to demonstrate his beliefs.

When we got to High Plains Baptist Hospital in Amarillo, my dad greeted me with one of those rare physical embraces that told me more than words.

What could I say when he told me, "Eighty-two good years and one bad week. I'll take that."

Three days later a hearse took him home to Borger, and McGee Street, and Calvary Baptist Church, and Virginia.

My little Irish mother, Nellena Gibson Dawson, had never had the constitution of my father. The years of taking in washing, six pregnancies, tuberculosis, and a fragile little body almost five feet tall all contributed to her death a decade before my father.

He was fortunate to find in Virginia a person with whom he could share his years. She was as good for him as he was for her.

The day after the funeral, the farewell was said to friends and family, and there were only Margie, Virginia, and me in the house we called home.

We all decided it would be good for everyone if Margie and I helped Virginia deliver funeral wreaths to a rest home in Keeler Heights.

Virginia had kept inside of her so many of the things she wanted to say but could not express. It was when we took the flowers into the rest home that she turned to us with a look on her face I had never seen before, and would not see again.

She said, "I do not want to live like those poor folks in there. If I had a choice, I would like to be somewhere having a chicken sandwich and then just go on to be with your daddy and the Heavenly Father."

It was half past ten as we drove away from the rest home. An hour later we were sitting in Virginia's favorite restaurant in Borger. She had just eaten half of a chicken sandwich and had folded a napkin around the remaining half and put it in her purse.

"There," she said. "That takes care of my dinner tonight. What are you going to do?"

Then Virginia leaned back in the booth, closed her eyes, and went to be with my father and her Heavenly Father.

The last legal act on behalf of the estate of Frank A. Dawson was the transfer of title for the house on 323 North McGee Street to Calvary Baptist Church.

The final spiritual act on behalf of the life of Frank A. Dawson was the invitation to enter into one of the mansions in the "Father's House" that had been under construction since the foundations of time were laid.

Uncalling the Called

There are those who adhere strongly to the belief that most pastor search committees are cleverly disguised remnants of the Keystone Cops.

Nothing puts on display the fallibility of human endeavors like the average group of folks who have accepted the responsibility to "go find us a preacher."

Fortunately for the prospective pastor, the close kin of committee members, and the local townspeople who place church folks on pedestals, most of the really funny elements of the pastoral search never experience the light of day.

A case in point involved the stately First Baptist Church of Wichita Falls. The pastor search committee concluded what must have seemed an interminable process by offering an invitation to Morris Chapman to come to the church for an intensive effort to determine the will of the Lord with reference to his services as the pastor.

Unknown to me was the fact that Dr. Chapman was invited to arrive on Monday after I was invited to preach at all of the Sunday services. The information gap was widened by the fact that no one on the pulpit supply committee was aware of the fact that I was not aware of the plans concerning Dr. Chapman.

When I arrived late Saturday night and claimed my motel reservation, the only information waiting for me at the desk was a note reminding me that the early service started promptly at 8:15 A.M. the next morning.

Things were further complicated by the fact that I arrived in Wichita Falls from the south just minutes before an ice storm blew in from the north, which gave a whole new meaning to the name "Trade Winds Motel."

By the time I was ready to make my way six or seven blocks to First Baptist Church on Sunday morning, I discovered that a sheet of ice made it virtually impossible for me to drive my car even that short a distance. I immediately set out for the church on foot and arrived at precisely the moment for the pulpit party and deacons to march into the early (8:15 A.M.) service.

Melvin Bradley saw me coming and motioned for me to "fall in line" as we made our way to the front of the temporary sanctuary. The main sanctuary was in the midst of extensive repairs.

All of this without an inkling on my part about what was to take place the next week.

I quickly learned that I was not the only uninformed person in First Baptist Church of Wichita Falls.

As soon as the platform party reached their appropriate places on the makeshift platform, and still without one word of information or introduction, one of the deacons stepped to the pulpit and commenced to lead the congregation in the morning invocation.

I am not sure his prayer startled the Lord, but it sure got my attention.

He thanked the Lord for bringing to the church the very man who was obviously qualified to lead the membership to a new chapter of commitment and service in Wichita Falls.

His prayerful concern was that everyone that day would have a clear message of affirmation and be ready to issue a call to become pastor of the church at an appropriate time.

Wo, Sally!

Or would Woe, Sally be more appropriate?

Unless my ears had deceived me, this fellow knew something I did not know.

Then he became more direct in his invocation of God's direct intervention and guidance. He asked for a clear and distinct sign that would convince everyone of the need for immediate action.

Maybe I had missed something in the mail.

I found myself somewhere between pre-stroke and pre-lightning bolt.

Just as I started to shift into a state my mother used to call a "hissy fit" I felt a tug on my arm. Bro. Melvin Bradley was leaning ever so slightly in my direction with a forefinger intruding into my rib cage.

"Not you! Not you! Not you!" he repeated.

It took a number of explanations, notes, giggles, red faces, and apologies to get through the service with any semblance of decorum.

I immediately learned a fundamental principle which governs all church communications. Information grows arithmetically, but ignorance grows geometrically. Desperation is the defining element in the latter case.

I have always been thankful that the Lord is not limited to actions which are based solely upon the information we provide.

Keep Looking Up

There is an old saying about never looking a gift horse in the mouth. We learned that you should never look a gift horse in the nose either.

The summer of 1968 was a time of transition for the

Dawson family. After eight years of service in the History Department of Wayland Baptist College we moved to Bryan/College Station where I was given the opportunity to help build the doctoral program in European History at Texas A&M University.

It was an indirect move, for I had previously accepted an appointment as visiting professor at Colorado State College (now University of Northern Colorado) for the summer term.

In the course of this wonderful summer of transition our family happened to be in downtown Denver for an afternoon of sightseeing and relaxation. As we walked past the Brown Palace Hotel we noticed that barricades were up and "Fourth of July" stuff was hanging from the lampposts. A band was playing, and a crowd was gathering in front of a large flatbed trailer in the middle of the block.

It took a number of unsuccessful inquiries to finally produce a clue as to what was happening. Nelson Rockefeller was having a campaign rally there in a few minutes.

It was to be the final pre-convention appearance before he flew to Florida to try to capture the Republican Party's nomination for president of the United States.

It was like an appointment with destiny.

As we stood in front of the speaker's trailer we realized that by accident we had the best vantage point in the entire audience (which actually consisted of just us and a few other curious onlookers). A crowd materialized from nowhere as half of the team of Rowan and Martin appeared on the makeshift stage and began to warm up the crowd. Then the band played a rousing rendition of "Stars and Stripes Forever" as a motorcade made a timely entrance and proceeded to deliver the star of the show to the steps leading to the stage.

Free banners appeared from nowhere. Pictures, hats, whistles, and streamers all magically made their way into the hands of the Dawson family.

For once I glowed with the historical importance of the moment. And I could hardly escape the sense of achievement for bringing our Keystone 8 with us. It was one of those marvelous turret cameras with regular, wide, and telescopic lenses, and we were occupying the very best spot available for wonderful pictures. The only concern was about the fact that I did not have excess film left over in the camera.

As soon as Governor Rockefeller came to the microphone, I began to record the momentous event. I was looking up into his face from only eight feet away, and the trusty Keystone was rolling.

I could not have programmed my good fortune any better if I had been on the planning committee.

Excitement turned into pure giddiness when the governor responded to the adulation of the crowd, stepped around the podium, and reached directly past me to shake the hands of Margie, Kim, Carey, and Jamie. My camera was recording history at a mere yard or two away.

As quickly as the rally started, it was over with. After a brief prediction of victory in Miami and ultimate success in November, the party loaded up and headed out.

We were left with a feeling of victory. Carey, our middle son, gloried in his new poster. He said he would go home and put it on the wall if he only had a wall.

The rest of the family shared little artifacts which would serve as testimony to others that indeed we had actually shaken hands with the man who might be the next president of the United States.

And I had the most priceless footage anyone ever took. And it was all an unexpected gift.

Or so it seemed.

What we soon learned was that the turret of my camera had been turned to the telescopic lens.

I had managed to take priceless footage, to be sure. But it was priceless only because it was probably the only footage in the world looking up Nelson Rockefeller's nose!

Folks say one should never look a gift horse in the mouth. Add noses to the list.

Looking Beyond the Image

Shortly after joining the faculty of Wayland Baptist College in 1960, I taught a class in historiography. It was offered at night, and the targeted consumers were members of the professional class in the Plainview community.

Nearly twenty people signed up and most, if not all, were auditing the course. It was a pure delight. What I did not know at the time was that among those taking the course were many of the leaders of various women's study groups in and around Plainview. The relationship forged in this and succeeding classes led to a seven-year tenure as guest lecturer for several of the clubs on a regular basis.

It was sheer joy to watch as these fine students of history began to practice the art as well as the science of history.

"Start looking where you are," they were told, "for history is all around you."

Plainview was still populated by people who were the first settlers on the land on which they lived. Once the students realized that the makers of the history of this part of Texas were still alive, and in full possession of their faculties, the walk back into the past became a stampede.

One Friday afternoon in 1961 I witnessed one of the first fruits of historical inquiry. A former student of that first seminar and a regular participant in one of the local study clubs called me with the news that she had started looking "where she was."

The result of her quest was the rediscovery of an old portrait in the attic.

Would it be possible for her professor to come to her home and take a look at the painting?

Some family collectibles are historical. Some are hysterical. The portrait belonged in the latter category.

After complimenting my friend for initiating a search, I had to be honest with her and tell her that I was fearful that the painting was without redeeming value except for the purpose of name recognition of a deceased relative. Her immediate reaction was to admit that it had been a long shot at finding some fabulous rare work worth a small fortune.

After a brief moment of disappointment, I moved on to the subject that intrigued me more than the portrait of some dear departed uncle. Had she noticed the unique nature of the frame? After all, the corollary to "look around you" is "look beyond what you see around you."

With her permission, we turned to the back of the frame and began the tedious process of taking the back off of the wooden frame.

What we found excites me to this day.

There, behind the old painting, was one of the original copies of the Articles of Secession for the State of Alabama.

After a few calls to the proper offices in Alabama, a rare and priceless historical artifact found its way "home."

Her testimony to her study club the next Tuesday remains with me to this day.

- Surely enough, there are treasures all around us, waiting for earnest and proper evaluation.
- Indeed, man looks to the outside and God looks to the inside to find the true value in each of us.
- The lost sheep are certainly worth the attention of the shepherd, even when they appear to be black sheep.
- Behind even the poorest of reproductions of man there may be found something worth keeping.

Look Inside Yourself

I can recall only a few events from my year in the fourth grade at West Ward in Borger. Grades two and three abound with memories, and grade five abounds with numerous events that come to mind on a regular basis.

One of those few mental pictures that stay with me from the fourth grade relates to my two sisters.

Barbara, three years my elder, fell victim to diabetes and

ultimately went to be with the Lord at age thirty-six as a result of the toll it took upon her body.

Nella, three years younger than I, was always in good health, but constantly lived in the shadow of Barbara's sickness.

We all had photographs taken on about the same day at West Ward. Barbara looked well and healthy in her picture. Nella, on the other hand, had developed sores on her mouth the day before her picture was taken and my little mother/doctor had treated her with some purple-colored concoction that looked almost black in the picture.

Barbara kept her picture for years, remembering the time of the picture as the time "when I still felt good."

Nella kept her picture, too, but always remembered it as the time "I was sick and Mother made me well."

Such a trivial event hardly seems to warrant an allocation of memory cells, but each of the three of us remembered the same day for different reasons. It always comes back to me when I read the story in the Gospel of John regarding the healing of the blind man who stood in front of the Temple.

Some looked back and remembered him as the one who had been blind. Jesus remembered him as the man who was able to see.

The blind man himself said he once was blind, but now he could see. He suggested that, perchance someone wanted to know more about it, maybe they should talk to Jesus.

Look to Jesus

It was near the end of the fall term at East Texas Baptist College, and the time of year for students to begin to panic just a little bit because of bills, absences, engagements, basketball, and Christmas, to name only a few.

Most of the problems were related to time or money. Occasionally there were difficulties at home that had filtered through the veil to the campus and cast a shadow over things. Many times there was plain old loneliness that could only be alleviated by a few home-cooked meals and a good hug from Mother.

In this particular case, Mary came into my office with tear-filled eyes and a hand written letter in her purse.

It had all of the earmarks of a "two-tissue-box of tears" kind of visit. Mary tried a number of times to tell me what had brought her to such a state of personal distress, but she simply could not utter three words without breaking into tears.

Finally she reached into her purse and brought out a letter which she seemed almost afraid to touch. Placing it on the desk between us, Mary tenderly pushed the envelop across to me and pulled back while I opened it for myself.

In all of my years of reading communications, I have to say that this was the worst letter I have ever read.

It was from Mary's father. He recounted how he and her mother had opposed her wish to enroll at ETBC. He said that he had been fearful that she would get "involved" in religious "stuff" at the school and prove to be an embarrassment to her family.

It seems that she had come home for Thanksgiving and shared her profound experience of faith with her parents, confirming their worst fears about her stay at "that school" in Marshall.

He said that he had given it much thought and felt that it would be best for everybody if she did not come home for Christmas. It would obviously be too much of an embarrassment to everyone concerned if she were there.

Then, in a grand gesture of arrogance, he added that since this Jesus was such a friend of hers, perhaps He should help pay the remainder of her school bills, for he and her mother no longer felt obligated to do so.

It was signed, "Your Father."

The letter was beyond belief. Mary's father was disowning his daughter because of her new-found faith!

I had heard accounts of tribes in the jungle that expelled members who had professed faith, and Communist regimes withdrawing all benefits from believers, but never anything like this.

As I lowered the letter and looked toward Mary I must have been a pretty bad example of Christian brotherhood. My first statement just slipped out.

"THIS IS AWFUL!"

That was not what Mary had come to my office to hear. She already knew that it was awful.

"Oh, Dr. Dawson," she cried, "what am I to do?"

It was at that moment that the weight of my answer to her became unbearable. I had been through church, Sunday School, Training Union, Win Schools, camps, retreats, revivals, January Bible Studies, Glorietta Encampment, two Baptist colleges, doctoral studies, and an army physical during the Korean War. I suddenly realized that none of these had prepared me for a glib answer to the most profound problem of Mary's life.

All I could do was pray a silent but heart-felt prayer that whatever I said would help.

"What do you want to do?" was all I could muster.

Back came the most mature and challenging confession I have ever heard, anywhere, from anybody.

"I just want to do what Jesus wants me to do," she uttered before she gave way to another episode of tears.

> Whether we look upward, inward, outward, or backward, we must someday look to Jesus to determine the important alternatives of our lives.

Mary and her family finally came to a resolution of the tensions wrought from her faith and her walk of Christian obedience. Only the Father can judge the eternal consequences.

One truth has stayed with me from the experience with Mary.

Whether we look upward, inward, outward, or backward, we must someday look to Jesus to determine the important alternatives of our lives.

Heart for Heart

What is better than having six bypasses in December of 1993?

Surviving the surgery in 1994!

I have met two folks who have had seven, and three who have had six. The fact of the matter is, most folks who are in need of that much heart surgery do not last long enough to share the experience with others.

Just about everything about your personal lifestyle undergoes the closest scrutiny.

For instance, what can you eat?

"Simple," says my doctor. "If it tastes good, spit it out!"

Weight control, prescribed exercise programs, avoidance of fatigue, and avoidance of crowds all take on the aura of command performances. Without becoming morbid about it, even the simplest of daily activities take on the nature of crisis management.

In the midst of the reorientation of lifestyles there occurs an interesting desire to talk with others who can share their post operative experiences. Some surgical veterans refer to it as the "zipper club" because of the characteristic scar left on the chest and down the right leg.

The zipper club, and its potential for spiritual witness, came into play on a Partnership Missions trip to New South Wales, Australia.

We were in the middle of a week of evangelistic services at Wollongong Baptist Church, a wonderful fellowship under the very capable pastoral care of Rev. John and Judith Taylor. I had felt "at home" from the very first service in the church because of the similarities between Australia and Texas.

Like Texas, Australia is populated by immigrants from virtually every country in the world. Friendships are quickly and easily forged. The requirements for survival cause folks to develop a quick wit and a ready willingness to share very private elements of their lives.

Helmut, a native of East Germany, had immigrated to New South Wales as a child after World War Two.

He had endured an incredible experience when his family was caught between the lines of retreating Germans and advancing Russians during the last weeks of the war. The suffering he had experienced as a result of the succeeding weeks of dislocation and despair had given Helmut an unusual empathy for those in need.

Helmut's natural empathy led him to share with me a grave concern he had for Werner, his neighbor. Like himself, the neighbor was a relocated German.

Helmut explained that his neighbor was suffering from heart problems that seemingly could not be diagnosed. A very private individual, his neighbor had retreated into a state of isolation and despair.

It was Helmut's hope that our common bond of heart problems might open the door for us to share more than just our hearts.

Werner was a very impressive individual. His educational credentials included a doctorate in architectural engineering from the University of Leipzig. His German was the classic "high German" so typical of professional educational circles.

I shared with Werner my medical history and explained to him the path that had led from danger to physical well-being.

It was at that point that Werner asked if he might confide in me. After I assured him that I would treat his confidences with the utmost care, he shared with me an incredible story based on his educated opinion that he was a victim of the practice of witchcraft.

To the best of my knowledge this was the one and only time in my life that I have talked with anyone who believed himself to be the victim of witchcraft. I somehow had always associated the belief in witches with ignorance and poverty.

Werner was convinced that those closest to him, in family circles in particular, were slowly but surely driving him to certain death from what would appear to be natural heart problems. He seemed absolutely convicted that he was doomed to die by means of diabolical forces which he could not resist.

I was overwhelmed by the implications of the scripture that said, "As a man thinketh in his heart, so is he."

Correctly or incorrectly, I likened Werner's plight to that

of all lost people in general and mine in particular. And even the mention of heart surgery was terrifying to him.

I shared with him that he might consider the possibility of a new heart from the Great Physician.

Only after being equipped with a spiritual new heart would Werner be able to withstand the forces of this world, whatever those forces might be or might seem to be. And the best way to deal with a new heart would be for him to find fellowship with others who had already undergone the experience themselves.

Would it be hard to take on a new nature? Not nearly as hard as the migration he and his family had endured as the result of war during his childhood.

One does not always get to see the end result of the planting of a seed. It took a year for news to reach me by way of Wollongong friends that Werner had experienced a miraculous reversal of the downward trend in his health. He had found a source of fellowship in a local Lutheran congregation. He seemed in control of his life.

I wonder if anybody in Wollongong refers to Werner and his friends as a spiritual zipper club.

Folks in need of this type of treatment seem especially encouraged to see folks who appear to have passed the test with flying colors and have resumed a normal lifestyle.

I still ponder the irony of the circumstances which led to a post operative trip to Australia, which resulted in a witnessing opportunity with a "heart-sick immigrant from Germany."

Pardons, Pickups, and Pianos

Tommy Dale Tucker and Jerry Dawson were a dangerous combination of fifteen-year-olds.

Tuck had access to his step-father's old pickup that he used in his trade as a plumber. Tuck's problem was the absence of a driver's license.

I had access to the highways of Texas by way of an emergency license due to the poor health of my sister, Barbara. The only vehicle available to me was our 1937 Plymouth with a very limited reliability threshold.

We both should have known better (sounds familiar, doesn't it?), when we were approached by the operator of a local music store.

He (alias Mr. Smith) wanted us to help him move two pianos to Borger from a garage in Amarillo, fifty miles away. Using Tuck's pickup and my talents as a driver (with license in hand), we could earn $10 each for three hours of work, which was not bad in 1947. Mr. Smith would accompany us to relieve any parental apprehensions that might arise.

It never seemed to dawn upon anyone that there might be something a little "strange" about the whole operation. Why would a reputable businessman hire two "kids" with a beat up old pickup to move his valuable merchandise late on Saturday night?

Before the night was over there would be a long series of questions added to the list.

Getting to Amarillo and picking up the two upright pianos proved to be easy enough. Covering the two instruments with tarps and pulling onto Northeast Eighth traffic, we encountered our first problem.

The weight of the pianos caused the headlights to shine almost straight up. Every car we met repeatedly flashed its dimmer. When I responded with my dimmer, it only lowered the beams enough to shine directly into the eyes of the oncoming vehicle.

Each and every car we met on the way to Panhandle repeated the dimming ritual, and some added a verbal communication as they went by.

By the time we turned north toward Borger, I was getting a little irritated at the bad manners and insults coming my way, irrespective of the fact that I was the cause of all the problems.

As we passed the gate to the 6666 Ranch, an irate driver added a new element to the dim-bright-dim-routine. He turned on a spotlight and almost blinded us. I barely noticed as we went by that the car was black and white. I thought only Department of Public Safety patrol cars were painted like that.

I also noted through my rear view mirror that the vehicle seemed to be turning around at the old Gulf Oil camp. Strange.

Then we topped the long straightaway next to the carbon black plants south of Borger, and I got the impression that things were about to get a little bumpy for the Dawson/Tucker express.

Across the highway and on both sides were what seemed to be a policemen's convention. Five or six DPS patrol cars, representatives from the Hutchinson County Sheriff's Department, and a Texas Ranger were there. I could have sworn that the members of the reception committee were all holding rifles.

My first impression was that this was a pretty tacky reaction to some bright headlights. It also struck Mr. Smith as a little unusual. He turned to me and said that those pianos we were hauling belonged to me.

At that point I stopped at the roadblock across the highway, rolled down my window, and commenced one of those valuable lessons from the book of life.

Several sets of spotlights illuminated the cab as a very polite DPS officer asked to see my driver's license.

"Son, what do you have under the tarp?" he asked, this time not so politely.

I got the strange feeling that things were headed south for the Dawson/Tucker express.

"Pianos," I managed to squeak out of a suddenly inoperative throat.

"Do you mind if we take a look?" he asked. Well, he didn't actually *ask*. It was more like a command. At any rate, it must have seemed like a lot of fun, because he was joined by several officers who shared his inordinate interest in pianos.

It only took a minute for six patrolmen to peel back the canvas tarp and verify the fact that indeed we were hauling two pianos.

"Whose pianos are they?" he asked.

After a nudge in my right rib cage from Mr. Smith, I inaccurately replied that they belonged to my father.

"What does your father do for a living?" he asked.

"He is a welder for J. M. Huber Corporation in Borger."

"Isn't he a farmer?"

"No sir. He is a welder."

"Then what is he doing with farm license tags on this pickup?"

At that point I gagged. I had gotten myself into a mess so bad that I knew I was about to be handcuffed and taken to jail where I would break rocks for the rest of my life.

Then the officer got "in my face" as the current saying goes.

"Son, you are the luckiest young man alive. We don't have time to mess with you right now, so get this pickup out of here. And don't ever pull a stunt like this again, whatever it is you are doing."

Two days later there was a story in the paper about a Saturday night shoot-out between law enforcement officers and some bootleggers south of Borger. The incident occurred at a roadblock which had been set up to intercept a load of whiskey being transported in an old pickup.

The officers evidently had been tipped ahead of time that the fellows carrying the illegal shipment were pretty bad hombres. The heavily armed welcoming committee was fully prepared to shoot first and ask questions later.

When I look back on the experience I see how similar it was to the daily encounters we have with the world of our Heavenly Father.

It is dangerous business to be a sinner in the hands of an angry God. What strikes us as harmless violations and naïve decisions have the potential of bring-

> What strikes us as harmless violations and naïve decisions have the potential of bringing us to the point of gross violations of God's redemptive plan.

ing us to the point of gross violations of God's redemptive plan.

Getting into trouble is a whole lot easier than getting out. Ask Adam.

And none of life's stories end up with a free pass home without answering first to the divine judgment of the Father.

I Am a Jelly Roll

Great moments that capture the imagination of a worldwide audience are rare, usually spontaneous, and quite often short lived.

In spite of the public relations efforts of politicians to attract and retain the attention of the public, the media, and voters, only rarely does a single sentence or phrase achieve a form of historical immortality.

Roosevelt's reference to December 7, 1941, as a day that would live in "infamy," Churchill's "Finest Hour" declaration, MacArthur's promise, "I shall return!' are examples with which we are all familiar.

Immortal statements do not have to have internal coherence or grammatical qualities.

John F. Kennedy made a speech in Berlin that did more to enhance his relationship with Europe than almost any event in his administration.

He pointed to the Berlin Wall and proudly proclaimed, *"Ich bin ein Berliner."*

What he said and what he meant were two entirely different things.

An accurate translation would be, "I am a jelly roll." *Ein Berliner* was the name of a popular pastry. *Berliner* would refer to his citizenship as a resident of the city.

It was not the grammar that brought a tumultuous response from a million oppressed people. It was the heart behind the words. No history of the turning points and crucial moments of the Cold War will ever be complete without some reference to Kennedy's speech that day.

And while the world may not be paying undivided attention with immortalizing pen in hand to record what we say, somebody is listening. What preacher has not responded to a report on his sermon with something like "I said *What?*"

Who among us has not, at some critical moment, said one thing and meant another?

Many of us have had an experience like that of a committee from the Division of Student Work of the Baptist General Convention of Texas. The committee had met in Irving and completed work in time for a bite to eat at a local restaurant. Jack Greever and Jan Daehnert were deeply engrossed in debate over the minutes of the meeting when a waiter came by with the standard two pots of coffee.

The waiter had the look of a newcomer to Irving, to Texas, and to the United States.

Few natives of Irving smile that big, and few waiters in Texas are that eager to serve your every whim.

He stopped beside Jan and held out the two pots of coffee, obviously waiting for him to select "regular" or "decaf."

What our newly arrived immigrant to the United States could not possibly have known was that Daehnert drank only Sanka. Every one of the regulars at the business knew this.

When the waiter proffered the two pots for Daehnert's choice, Jan turned and very politely asked, "Sanka?"

Immediately our waiter smiled an even bigger smile than before and said, "Ju welcome."

While not on the grand scale of Kennedy's pronouncement, the waiter's response simply adds another dimension to the possibility of multiple interpretations to our words.

Our words with the Father are not left to multiple interpretations. And our words with the Father are more eternal than the famous quotations from Churchill or Roosevelt. The scriptures tell us that every thought, every word, every deed is recorded in the Heavenly Record. How fortunate we are that the Father not only keeps a record of what we say, but also what our heart is saying.

Character or Characters?

The list of great tragedies to strike Texas in the twentieth century is long and painful.

Who can forget the terrible hurricane that struck Galveston Island, or the Texas City explosion? The boll weevil infestations of the 1920s? The drought from 1952 to 1957? Or the terrible football teams at Plainview in the 1960s?

It has been bad enough to always live in Texas towns with limited dining facilities, Hart Hanks newspapers, populations of about 25,000, and poor football programs.

In Plainview we were witness to one of the longest football streaks in Texas high school history.

We were treated to a losing streak of twenty-eight games. One tie game kept the record from being thirty-five in a row.

At what had to be the low point for the school, the team, the coaches, and the community, the squad for the last game of one of the losing seasons was only seventeen players.

Ask any fan of the game about those four terrible seasons and it might surprise you what they remember more than anything else.

They remember Lawrence McCutcheon and Jerry Sisemore. Two of the great names from the American sports scene were participants in the worst string of games in modern Texas football history.

McCutcheon went from the backfield of Plainview to the All-Pro ranks of the NFL by way of Colorado State University. Jerry Sisemore repeatedly earned All-Pro honors over nearly two decades as the league's stellar guard, an honor for which he seemed destined while a star of the University of Texas line.

I must confess that I never had the opportunity to become acquainted with either of these young men while we were all there together. I do not know enough about their personal lives to recommend them as role models.

I do know that I personally have always been moved by their ability to rise above what seemed a hopeless environment to achieve the highest accolades of their peers.

I sometimes liken their example to the Disciples in the Garden, at the trial of Jesus, and the Crucifixion. There was ample reason to assume that the team had lost, but their personal commitment to the cause paramount in their lives was enough to make them heroes of the faith.

It all speaks to the difference between being a character in life's dramas or having the character to face life's dramas.

You Took the Wrong Plane, Didn't You?

One should always be wary of good deals, shortcuts, or spur-of-the-moment decisions. That goes double for air travel.

It is hard enough to stay out of trouble with a fixed schedule and clear-cut destinations. Throw in a last minute change, and it almost guarantees a bad mistake on the part of somebody.

I was on my way to gate seventeen at Love Field in Dallas to catch a Southwest flight to Hobby in Houston. A meeting involving two dozen people had been simplified by reserving a meeting room at the terminal, minimizing the possibility for missed connections, and cutting expenses for taxis and car rentals.

To make sure that Murphy's law did not enter into the equation, I had allowed an extra hour in case traffic became a problem in getting to the airport. This destined me to sit for an hour at gate seventeen.

As I walked past gate three, the gate attendant announced the last call for a Houston flight and urged any late-comers to board in the next minute or so.

Never one to pass up a golden opportunity, I presented my ticket to him and asked if it might be possible to move my flight up by one hour and board his flight.

"Not a problem," he answered.

The prospect of extra time at Hobby and the possibility of fellowship with other members of the team gave me a warm glow of unanticipated satisfaction. There is nothing as comforting as beating the system.

Imagine the consternation I experienced when the Southwest flight landed right on time at **Houston International**.

It had never dawned on me to check the destination of the flight.

Big mistake!

I was about to land forty miles from Hobby International. Time-wise I would be farther from my destination than when I got on the plane in Dallas.

I felt so dumb!

The only good I could find in the predicament was the fact that Margie was not with me. No husband wants to give his wife that kind of material to work with.

Then a light came on.

There surely would be a shuttle service between Houston International and Hobby. I was an hour early, and with any luck I could make it to the meeting without having to publish to the world that I had made such a colossal blunder.

Sure enough, a question or two at the information desk got me to the shuttle desk.

I nonchalantly approached the ticket agent and asked if there might be a shuttle any time soon to Hobby?

He just smiled, winked at me, and proclaimed for everyone to hear, "TOOK THE WRONG PLANE, DIDN'T YOU?"

If you think it is embarrassing to make a bad decision about an earthly destination, ponder a bit about the day when all of our bad choices about our Heavenly destination will be read to us before the Father and the Heavenly Host.

No one would want to take a shuttle to an alternate terminal under those circumstances.

Hiding Behind the Tassels

The year 1964 marked a profound change in general policy and practice for the University of Texas. In its illustrious history that institution had never conferred an honorary doctorate. That policy was changed with the announcement that both Lyndon Baines Johnson and Lady Bird Johnson would be so honored during spring commencement ceremonies in Austin.

The announcement was met with everything from applause to anger. Lady Bird Johnson might have been a legitimate candidate for recognition, being a graduate of the school, but President Johnson had never been identified with the Forty Acres like Lady Bird had. He made a point to inform anyone who would listen that he was a graduate of "the normal school in San Marcos" only thirty miles to the south.

When he became president by way of the vice-presidency and the tragic assassination of John F. Kennedy, the very liberal student leadership on the UT campus somehow blamed Johnson. Other segments on the campus had never forgiven Johnson for accepting the vice-presidency to begin with.

The Daily Texan, the student newspaper, became the filter through which all of the various forms of protest passed. The closer the date came for the ceremony, the louder and nastier the letters, articles, and editorials became.

I was a microcosm of the feelings of the larger community of students and scholars.

I was to receive my degree of doctor of philosophy at the ceremony honoring the president and the first lady. Early on I sensed that the entire affair had the potential of becoming a public relations fiasco. I had a deep foreboding that "my" proud moment would somehow become lost in the shuffle of presidential public relations.

At the same time, I felt that I should consider myself fortunate to be part of an undeniably historical moment. Little did I realize that I was going to be given a post-graduate crash course in pure platform magic.

The ceremony got off to a rocky start. Planned as an open air event in front of the tower, the entire event had to be relocated across Town Lake to the Convention Center when a front brought Mother Nature's worst to bear on the campus.

Late, wet, and cramped into makeshift facilities, a very hostile crowd focused attention on the podium as the time arrived for the president of the United States to speak prior to the granting of degrees. One could actually feel the animosity of the audience when he was presented.

President Lyndon Baines Johnson went directly to the task at hand. He said that prior to coming to Austin he had been reading old issues of *The Daily Texan*. Perhaps the audience might like to know some of the comments people had made about the president of the United States.

With that, he began reading directly from a sheath of clippings. These citations accused the chief executive of everything from war mongering to animal cruelty. Over and over the readers were reminded of the president's obvious faults and failures.

The more he read, the quieter it got. Two minutes into the recitation, it was as though all of the air had been sucked out of the auditorium.

Platform guests started looking for a banner behind which they might hide.

The faculty and administration began to sink into their chairs, almost as though they were hoping for a brief demonstration of "the rapture." I could have sworn that some were actually trying to hide behind their tassels.

Still the president went on. After a few minutes that seemed like a week, President Johnson paused.

Yes, those were excerpts from *The Daily Texan* . . . **when Teddy Roosevelt visited Austin**.

Then he lowered his reading material, peered characteristically over his glasses, and said, playfully, "Why, you didn't think they were talking about me, did you?"

It took a minute, but the reaction started with a titter here, a laugh there, then more. Thirty seconds later the entire audience was laughing.

They had been had.

Another thirty seconds saw the audience rise to a standing ovation. Even the faculty came out from behind their tassels.

I had seen a pro in action. President Johnson had turned an absolutely hostile audience into a cheering crowd in less than three minutes.

If this seems impressive, consider the life of Jesus which made it possible for us to break down the wall of enmity between each of us and the holiness of the Father. We move from the realm of enemies of God to become sons of His, and joint-heirs with Jesus.

For Fishermen Only

It was late August 1968.

My summer appointment as visiting professor of History at Colorado State Teachers College (now University of Northern Colorado) had run its course. Margie and the kids had already left Greeley for College Station and Texas A&M University while I stayed behind to wrap up the semester.

My last afternoon in Colorado was devoted to a new joy in my life—trout fishing.

I made my way up the *Poudre* to Chambers Lake where *Los Pinos* flows into that magnificent body just below the continental divide.

I had the lake almost to myself. Occasional large snowflakes the size of silver dollars settled on the otherwise still water as I rigged up for one last and very private afternoon.

I was using a Zebco 33 with two-pound test which was attached to a medium bubble half-filled with water. A nine-foot, two-pound-test leader was tipped with a No. 16 Gray Hackle Peacock which I was fishing wet.

About an hour into my treasured solitude, I heard a car stop about a hundred yards away. Thirty minutes (and two fourteen-inch rainbows) later, I heard the car door close.

After my third catch-and-release, I was joined by a gentleman in his fifties who was wearing dress clothes and a pleading expression.

It seems that he was at the end of a vacation and was about to go back to Dallas where he held a very responsible position with the Santa Fe Railroad. He had noted my Texas tags on my car. He had also noted with interest that I seemed to be pretty successful in catching trout.

Would it be possible for me to show him how to catch trout?

I myself had asked that question of a fellow history prof at Greeley only two months before. I had the debt of all fishermen to pass on to others what had been given to me.

When I asked him if he had fishing tackle with him, he beamed like a little child. Up the embankment he ran, unmindful of the beating his dress shoes were taking.

As he got near his car I saw the window come down on the passenger side. Although I could not hear just exactly what his wife was saying from a hundred yards away, there was enough smoke to convince me there was a fire in the car.

None of these little annoyances stopped him. Like a little child about to play with a wonderful new toy, he made his way back to the bank of Chambers Lake and proudly presented to me the worst set of fishing tackle I had ever seen.

For starters, it was an open-faced heavy duty bass rig with what looked like twenty-pound test steel wire for line. Everything was coated with a layer of rust. My initial impression was that he had not been fishing in five or six years.

From the start I felt like it would never be possible for him to use the fly-and-bubble technique with his rig, but the look in his eyes told me that this was one of those golden moments in his life.

To prepare him for what seemed imminent failure, I told him that the technique I used was pretty tricky. Maybe it would be best for me to rig him up and then have a few practice casts to make sure I had done it correctly.

Assuring me that it must indeed be a rather tricky operation, he gave his undivided attention and a promise to remain in my debt "forever" if I could only help him catch his first trout.

I let out a little line, slowly reeled in, and then repeated the cast, adding a few feet each time. Before each cast, which I assumed would be the final cast before his rusty rig locked up in tangles, I assured my eager student that this casting business was "pretty tricky."

Finally, the moment of truth; a date with destiny; the point of no return; all or nothing!

With my left foot in *Los Pinos* and my right foot in Chambers Lake, I cast the line and bubble. Boy, did I cast the line and bubble! The first thirty yards of line let out as smoothly as one could want.

Then came disaster. The line snagged in the reel, jerking the line, bubble, leader, and fly abruptly to the left where the leader wrapped three or four turns around a bush on the edge of the lake.

It was only thirty yards away by line of sight. It was about a mile by foot back up *Los Pinos* and across, up a steep incline and around some rough terrain, and then down to the bush and our line.

The hard part was looking into the face of my new fishing dependent and seeing utter dismay written all over his face.

"Hey," I said, "Don't look so gloomy. This is all part of the tricky part of fishing for trout. What we have to do now is pull this line just right and it will come right back to us."

As far as I know, this was the only time I have asked for divine help on a fishing trip. And it was certainly going to take divine intervention to ever get that bubble, leader, and fly back to us. The only ray of hope was the fact that it was a twenty-pound test and could stand an enormous tug without breaking.

Ever so slowly I applied pressure until the rod was bent over double, the bush was leaning directly toward me, and the bubble was quivering up and down.

It was at that point that the leader started to unwind.

In a minute, everything turned loose and the two-ounce bubble shot back at us like a bullet, passing between the two of us, and pulling the leader and fly in tow.

Up the stream it went and, reaching the end of the line, settled on the water trailing the gray hackle peacock.

Pow!

The gray hackle peacock was taken out to lunch by a rainbow trout.

I am standing looking north, the line is pointing south, and the trout (with the gray hackle peacock in its jaw) darting east and west.

My student-turned-admirer-for-life seemed to have a holy glow about him as he reached over and touched my arm.

"That's some technique you got there."

In all humility I could only say, "Yes, and it works every time."

Mistaken Identity

I had the happy privilege of serving as dean of the Graduate School at Southwest Texas State University from 1971 to 1976.

The active files of the office contained records for over five thousand people who were in some stage of redirecting their lives or enhancing their chosen careers.

I was constantly amazed at the number of people who were successful in their professional careers but miserably unhappy with their life. When asked about their motivation for seeking admission to graduate school, perhaps fifty percent would point to the fact that their college careers had been "planned" for them since childhood.

Graduate studies offered their first real opportunity to redirect their professional and private lives.

In addition to this sizable group of college graduates, I have known any number of people whose college careers were outlined and planned **before** they were born.

As strange as it may seem, I do not recall ever discussing the possibility of attending college with my parents, my high school teachers, my counselors, my pastors, student recruiters, or anyone else until the very end of my senior year in high school. All of this was true in spite of the fact that I graduated fourth in a class of one hundred and seventy-seven.

Each of my parents had dropped out of school at the sixth grade, and neither ever seemed to know quite how to talk about a college education. I was always deeply moved at the profound confidence they both expressed at each and every decision I made as I worked my way through the doctoral level at the University of Texas. They supported us in any and every way they could, but they never felt competent to advise me in my educational endeavors. I never felt that either of them was lacking in their own special realm of good common sense.

In March of 1952, at the end of my senior year at Borger High School, all of this changed.

Jack Jeter and Bill Lewis came to Calvary Baptist Church for a youth revival. Both were students at Wayland Baptist College in Plainview.

During the concluding Sunday morning service of the revival I felt an overwhelming need to commit my life to "the ministry." Several young men responded in the same way, and there was a wonderful spirit in the church when the church voted to license us to the gospel ministry. That was pretty heady stuff for an eighteen-year-old.

Jack Jeter returned to Wayland and shared his experience at Calvary Baptist Church with Sam Choy, director of student work, who then made a personal visit to Borger to ask me to consider attending Wayland Baptist College in response to my call to the ministry.

Sam shared with President Bill Marshall his impressions of our visit together, and Dr. Marshall made a personal call to me and invited me to hear him speak in a nearby church. After I heard him speak, and visited with him following the service, there was not a hint of doubt about attending Wayland.

It is fair to say that unlike those many, many students whose college careers are planned from "Day One," mine remained unplanned almost to the day I enrolled.

The absence of advice was probably a blessing in disguise. When Margie and I were married on June 21, 1952, no one shared with us the magnitude of the obstacles that would await us as we made our way through school and marriage at the same time. No one in their right mind would have advised us to even dream of attempting undergraduate and graduate studies as we did.

Two events during our first day on campus shaped our collegiate experience from that day forward.

First, we moved our meager possessions into a fourteen-foot by fourteen-foot government surplus homette. The walls of these little huts were single sheets of plywood and barely held a bed, two easy chairs, a dinner table with chairs, and a small refrigerator and range.

When I began to unload all our worldly possessions into our homette, I was approached by a skinny fellow who introduced himself as Jimmy Morris from Mississippi. He noted that the refrigerator was too large for me to handle by myself and instructed me to give him a holler when I needed his help with it.

About a half-hour passed before I reached the point where I was ready to remove the refrigerator from the trailer. It seemed providential that just when I needed him again, Jimmy Morris suddenly appeared on the sidewalk in front of our homette. At least, he looked like Jimmy, sort of.

As soon as he said hello in that unmistakable Mississippi accent, I skipped the formalities and told him I was ready to move my refrigerator, and he was just in time to help.

Without so much as a word of dissent, he grabbed hold of his half of the refrigerator, and we moved it into place.

As soon as we were finished, I told him thanks and allowed as how he was free to go on about his business, which he did.

Only later in the day did I discover that there were two fellows of similar build with deep Mississippi accents. One was a student named Jimmy Morris, and the other was Ed MacMillan, head of the History Department.

A special bond was forged that day with Ed MacMillan as we moved my refrigerator. It was he who offered me a contract to fill a vacancy at Wayland in 1960 when I began my first career teaching assignment. Dr. MacMillan retired in 1998 after extended years of service as graduate dean at Mississippi College.

The colossal mistake I made with Ed MacMillan was followed in short order two hours later by another blunder of equal magnitude.

I was standing between the columns at the main entrance to Gates Hall, when I noticed two fellows moving a twelve-foot stepladder into position under one of the light fixtures hanging in front of the balcony. I could not remember ever seeing two less competent janitors in my life.

The only hope I could see for salvaging their jobs was for me to help them with a little organizational skill so that they could get the faulty light bulb replaced and get on about other things.

When I told them that it sure looked like they could use a little help and introduced myself as Jerry, they very courteously shook my hand and introduced themselves in turn as Orville and James.

I was eager for them to know that I did not look down upon janitors just because I was a student, but I did feel a sense of responsibility to point out to them that they needed to handle their light bulbs with a towel instead of with bare hands.

Imagine my embarrassment that evening at the reception for new students when I was greeted in the line by Orville Yeager, professor of History, and H. Preston James, dean of the college.

They laughed off the incident, but I shall never forget the servant spirit that led these two eminent scholars to fix what needed to be fixed, even if it meant that they would be mistaken for janitors.

In the course of my first year of study, each of the three historians I had met under the

> Every day of our life we encounter people who are in the process of realizing their potential to be all that God has endowed them to be.

worst of circumstances called me to a quiet place and asked me to consider the possibility of preparing myself to pursue doctoral studies and a collegiate teaching career and eventually an administrative career.

There is no telling what advice I might have gotten had I done things properly my first day on campus.

Every day of our life we encounter people who are in the process of realizing their potential to be all that God has endowed them to be.

The Oldest Church

The greatest barrier confronting students of history, outside of having football coaches who teach it because they have to teach something to keep on coaching, is the feeling of hopelessness in dealing with so much time.

After a few years of simply wading into ancient history, I finally concluded that it was worth half of a class to deal with the concept of time itself before dealing with events in time.

We all know someone who is at, or near, the age of one hundred. If we take the lives of two people that age and place their lives end to end, we would be back to the adoption of the constitution of the United States. Four lives in a row would take us back to the colony at Jamestown.

Five people like someone we know would take us back to the discoveries of Columbus.

Only nine lives would place us in the middle of the first Crusade.

Line up fifteen people, *only fifteen*, and we witness the Fall of the Roman Empire.

Nineteen lives would take us to the time Jesus walked on this earth.

It would take only forty-seven people to cover the entire period of the written record of man.

I had to laugh a little the first time we visited Brandenburg, seat of the Mark of Brandenburg who was one of the seven electors of the Holy Roman Empire. "New Town" (1191) was so named to distinguish it from "Old Town" (1171).

By contrast, I was born in Borger, Texas, on December 28, 1933. This was only seven years after Borger was born in 1926. As far as anyone knows, there is no "new" Borger.

My personal fixations about time and history help explain my excitement about a stop-over in Helsinki on a trip to Estonia. I had come across a map of the city illustrating the points of interest for travelers like me, and I was particularly attracted to a story about the "oldest church" in Helsinki.

Sensing the possibility of a good reference story for future use, I decided to place a visit to this historical church at the top of my very brief "must see" list.

I made my way on foot to the center of the district high-lighted in the travel magazine, only to find that there were several churches in the area and nothing in English to help me determine which of them might be my prize.

None of the people I questioned on the street seemed to know anything about the "oldest church" in Helsinki, and I was beginning to think that I had done a poor job of map reading. Finally, after falling back on German, I was able to get an elderly lady to talk with me.

Oldest church?

She turned and pointed in the direction of a small plaza and said it had been right over there.

Had been?

Yes. The church had been there. It had burned to the ground the year before.

"Wie schade," I exclaimed. (How sad)

With a twinkle in her eye, my new travel consultant replied that it did not create any problems.

"After all," she said, "we still have an oldest church in Helsinki."

Who Is Contacting You Now?

There are slices of our lives when all of the lines get blurred. Health problems, financial complications, career shifts, interpersonal relationships, to mention just a few, can sometimes all come to focus in a single moment. The result is that the usual avenues we take to solve problems just do not seem to lead anywhere.

My schedule for March 26-27, 1999, was routine enough.

Late in December 1998 Max Osborne called me on behalf of the deacons of First Baptist Church of El Paso. My services were requested for a deacon's retreat planned for March 27 at the church.

There were many positive sides to the invitation that caused me to agree to help out. As I shared with the men at the meeting, one of my earliest recollections stemmed from a Sunday afternoon in El Paso in December 1941.

Our family was visiting my Aunt Goldie, Aunt Edith, and Uncle Roy. We happened to be standing in front of a movie theater in the heart of the old center of town when two soldiers from Fort Bliss came running down the street while shouting that the Japanese had attacked Pearl Harbor.

Through the years my extended family in El Paso had kept in close contact through the services of my cousin Freddie Lee Reese (now deceased) and her husband John. Freddie was the volunteer church historian for First Baptist Church as well as keeper of the Family Tree for the Gibson clan.

Professionally, I had developed a twenty-five-year relationship with Dr. John Uxer by way of his service with the Christian Education Coordinating Board, his work as parliamentarian for the Baptist General Convention of Texas, and his educational career with the Regional Teacher Education Service Center in El Paso. I sensed that John was probably the source of the invitation to be part of the special weekend program.

Thus all of my impressions of the church, the pastoral staff, and deacon body had created in me a sense of admiration and respect. I was honored to be invited to join them for a special day of planning and preparation.

The week before I was to go to El Paso, the unexpected became the order of the day.

Margie became desperately ill. Abdominal pain and a whole list of adverse symptoms led to hospitalization and intensive efforts to diagnose the source of her problems.

Nothing emerged as the source of her difficulties, let alone a regime to follow in getting her well.

On the Tuesday before I was due to leave for El Paso on Friday, I was overwhelmed with a sense of indecision and confusion.

What should I do?

Should I call Dr. Levi Price, pastor of First Baptist Church, and tell him I might not be able to make the planned trip?

Should I wait another day or two in the hope that Margie would take a dramatic turn for the better?

Should I contact a possible substitute who could take my place and then offer the name to the church?

Standing alone in the entry hall of my home, I could not feel comfortable with any of the choices with which I felt confronted.

Then, as is so often the case with most of us, I sought some help from above. Surely the arrangements for the invitation and preparations for the trip, as well as the physical condition of my wife, were known by the Father.

Convinced that I did not need to supply background material to the Father, I simply confessed that I did not know what to do.

HELP!

Then came an answer. Call John Uxer.

That's it?

That's it!

I went to the phone and proceeded to dial 1-915-58, which was as far as I got. Before I could complete the dialing process, the phone began to make a strange clicking noise. Five clicks sounded, loud and clear, and then nothing. No ring, no disconnection.

Then a voice said, "Jerry?"

It was John Uxer. He had JUST DIALED MY NUMBER!

I do not understand the mechanics of the interface between his call to me and my dialing process, however incomplete it might have been. All I know is that we were dialing simultaneously.

John explained that he had felt a need to contact me and make sure everything was okay for my flight to El Paso on Friday and the retreat on Saturday.

Once I got the "goose bumps" to go away, I shared with John the nature of my dilemma.

Before he glibly offered some response, he prayed for wisdom. Then he suggested that we give the doctors and the great physician a little more time before we sought to find an answer to the problem facing us.

By Thursday, Margie had taken a decided turn for the better and for home and the quality of her health improved immeasurably. The trip to El Paso was amazingly uncomplicated, and the personal spiritual benefits I received from the experience far outweighed any good I might have done for the participants at the deacon's retreat.

And once again I had my faith in the Lord recharged with a demonstration of His omnipotence and His grace.

Without too much emphasis upon the "goose bump" aspect of our relationship with the Heavenly Father, I would encourage everyone to leave the line open for Him to "dial in."

Before we rush to judgment over life's complexities, we just might benefit from a call or two from Him.

And while we are at it, it might be worth remembering that God makes a lot of second-party calls, too. Have we received any of those lately?

A Grandfather's Postscript

Against almost unbearable pressure and an unrelenting surge of feelings of guilt, I have spared the readers of some "grandpaw stuff" that cried out to me for a page or two here and there.

For instance, I could have told about the evening Brandy, age four, sat in my lap and patiently listened as I read her some nursery rhymes. When I decided to sing some of these wonderful sources of entertainment, she turned to me and in absolute honesty and absent any malice, she said, "Pawpaw, you can't sing, can you?"

Or I could have yielded to the temptation and recalled Courtney's fourth Christmas with us when she unwrapped a clever foot-wide clock that was designed to teach children how to tell time. She excitedly hugged our necks and said, "Dis what I always wanted—a dwait big wist watch."

And surely I could have yielded again and related a visit made by Cara to the campus of East Texas Baptist University which was followed by a visit with her other grandparents in Canyon Lake. She was so proud that I was president. "President of what?" they asked. "Of the United States, of course."

And who would have faulted me for recounting the time Dawson referred to a story he had heard from the turn of the century as "Medieval times" and assured his friends that I knew about those things, because I was old.

Most grandfathers would surely understand if I shared Zachary's first fishing victory at the lake by our house. Like his grandfather taught him, he brought in a nice nine-inch catfish. Like his grandfather taught him, he removed the hook and returned the fish to the water. Like his grandfather taught him, he spread his little arms two feet wide when he told his grandmother how big it was.

And any grandmother would excuse me for Darby's loving question asked of Mrs. C. T. Bush shortly before her death from cancer. Sitting beside Mama Bush in church, Darby asked her dear, sweet, old friend if she were a Christian, adding, "That's important, you know."

And just maybe, parents and grandparents alike will understand the apprehension I felt when I asked Michael if there was anything he needed as he prepared to move into his college apartment. Likewise they will understand the sigh of relief I gave when Michael asked for an espresso machine. A grandson after my own adventuresome heart!

And who could fault me for remembering our quiet Emily. When asked what she wanted for Christmas, she vigorously responded, "PRESENTS. BUNCHES OF THEM."

Maybe it is best that I resist the urge to talk about my grandkids.